AN APPALACHIAN CURRICULUM

This project was sponsored through the Education Committee of the Appalachian Consortium by the following agencies:

The Blue Ridge Parkway

Pisgah National Forest

The Appalachian Trail Conference

East Tennessee State University

and

The Southern Appalachian Highlands Conservancy

Project Director: Patricia Lockamy, Blue Ridge Parkway
Coordinaors: Dr. Roberta Herrin, East Tennessee State University; Phyllis Honeycutt, Buncombe County Schools
Edited By: Susan Isaacs; East Tennessee State University
Art, Layout and Editorial Assistance By: Mary Ann Lawrence, Asheville, NC; Janet Kahler, Asheville, NC

Special Acknowledgments To:

Dr. Olson Huff, Pediatric Director, Ruth & Billy Graham's Children's Health Center, Asheville, North Carolina for his keynote address and expertise in the effects of the environment on children's health.

Emily Burleson of the Appalachian Consortium, who served as administrative coordinator for the project.

Joe DeLoach of the Tennessee Eastman Hiking Club, who helped coordinate funding.

Dr. Murray Evans of the Southern Appalachian Highlands Conservancy, who served as a primary instructor and guide for the project.

Terry Seyden, Public Affairs Officer for Pisgah National Forest, who helped coordinate funding and personnel.

The Appalachian Consortium was a non-profit educational organization composed of institutions and agencies located in Southern Appalachia. From 1973 to 2004, its members published pioneering works in Appalachian studies documenting the history and cultural heritage of the region. The Appalachian Consortium Press was the first publisher devoted solely to the region and many of the works it published remain seminal in the field to this day.

With funding from the Andrew W. Mellon Foundation and the National Endowment for the Humanities through the Humanities Open Book Program, Appalachian State University has published new paperback and open access digital editions of works from the Appalachian Consortium Press.

www.collections.library.appstate.edu/appconsortiumbooks

This work is licensed under a Creative Commons BY-NC-ND license. To view a copy of the license, visit http://creativecommons.org/licenses.

Original copyright © 1995 by the Appalachian Consortium Press.

ISBN (pbk.: alk. Paper): 978-1-4696-4244-4
ISBN (ebook): 978-1-4696-4245-1

Distributed by the University of North Carolina Press
www.uncpress.org

INSTRUCTORS FOR AN APPALACHIAN CURRICULUM

Robert Cherry
Resource Management Specialist, Blue Ridge Parkway

Ed Clark:
Habitat Manager, Grandfather Mountain

Dave Danley
Botanist, United States Forest Service

Dr. Murray Evans:
Professor Emeritus and Botanist, University of Tennessee

Dr. Roberta Herrin
Associate Professor of English, East Tennessee State University

Phyllis Honeycutt
Buncombe Coounty Schools

Marti Kane
Director of Programs and Education, North Carolina State Parks

Patricia Lockamy
North Carolina Interpretive Specialist, Blue Ridge Parkway

Lillian McElrath
Resource Management Specialist, Blue Ridge Parkway

Steve Miller
Park Ranger, Grandfather Mountain

Frank Roth
Operations Assistant, Pisgah National Forest

John Sharpe
Superintendent, Mt. Mitchell State Park

Steve Shupe
Park Ranger, Mt. Mitchell State Park

An Appalachian Curriculum is a product of the Appalachian Curriculum Summit, a week-long teacher workshop held on the campus of Appalachian State University in June, 1995. The purpose of the workshop was to allow children from the Southern Appalachian region to gain better educational access to the tremendous resources in this area. The project targeted fourth-grade teachers because they are in an advantageous position to influence children to be environmentally conscious and because fourth-grade curricula are compatible with the goals of the project. However, the activities produced may be adjusted for any age group.

During the workshop, the teachers visited four focal sites: The Blue Ridge Parkway, Grandfather Mountain, Mt. Mitchell, and Roan Mountain, including a portion of the Appalachian Trail. These sites were chosen because they contain some of the most environmentally significant areas in the Appalachian Highlands and because they are accessible to school groups in both western North Carolina and eastern Tennessee. At each site, the teachers were met by experts who guided them through an examination of the major environmental concerns, such as beaver dams along the Parkway, water quality at Linville Falls, and acid deposition and insect damage on Mt. Mitchell. On Roan Mountain and the Appalachian Trail, they explored the need for balance between public use and protection of rare and endangered species.

The results of their research and explorations are presented here, as An Appalachian Curriculum, a guide written for teachers, by teachers. The activities presented may be copied and used by any class or group who wishes to learn more about the resources of the Southern Appalachian region. The intent is that An Appalachian Curriculum will encourage other teachers to take advantage of these tremendous resources, and use them as living classrooms for their students.

ABOUT THE AUTHORS

The activities in An Appalachian Curriculum were written by seven teachers from the Appalachian region in North Carolina and Tennessee. They were all chosen for the project due to their experience in teaching in the region and their records for excellence in the classroom. The authors include:

Lisa Gibson - Mrs. Gibson is a fourth-grade teacher at Isaac Dickson Elementary School in Asheville, North Carolina. She is a graduate of Mars Hill College and has worked for Asheville City Schools for over seven years. She is also an experienced preschool teacher who is locally noted for excellence in the classroom. Mrs. Gibson resides with her husband and two children in Asheville.

Catherine Glenn - Mrs. Glenn serves as a teacher at Fairmont Elementary School in Johnson City, Tennessee. She holds a bachelors degree from Illinois State University and a Masters in Education from East Tennessee state University. She has been recognized as the Tennessee Association of Middle Schools Teacher of the Year (1993). Mrs. Glenn also received a national award from Keep America Beautiful in 1991.

Phyllis Honeycutt - A member of the Appalachian Consortium Education Committee who helped coordinate this project, Mrs. Honeycutt also has twenty-nine years of teaching experience in the Appalachian region. She has written several interdisciplinary curriculum guides. Mrs. Honeycutt is a resident of Mohawk, Tennessee and received her Bachelors degree from Mars Hill College and has completed graduate work at Western Carolina and Appalachian State Universities.

Cindy Medlock - Mrs. Medlock is a teacher at Black Mountain Primary School in Black Mountain, North Carolina, with twenty years of classroom experience. She also has over twenty-five years of experience as a seasonal park ranger with the Blue Ridge Parkway. She received her bachelors and masters degrees in education from Western Carolina University.

Diana Pennington - Mrs. Pennington is a fourth-grade teacher at Mountain City Elementary School in Mountain City, Tennessee, with over eight years of classroom experience. She holds a masters of arts in teaching degree from East Tennessee State University. She is active in school and community activities and sponsors an award winning 4-H club in Mountain City.

Karen Purcott - Karen teaches at Fairmont Elementary School in Johnson City, Tennessee and holds a masters degree from East Tennessee State University. She was named the Tennessee Social Studies Teacher of the Year in 1990. Karen has worked on previous curriculum projects in math and social studies and has developed and directed outdoor programs for the Girl Scouts.

Crystal Chapman - Mrs. Chapman is a fourth-grade teacher at Johnston Elementary School in Buncombe County, North Carolina, where she was recently named the 1995-96 Johnston Elementary Teacher of the Year. She is a graduate of Brevard College and The University of North Carolina at Asheville.

Mary Chandler - Mary is a senior at North Carolina State University. She participated in the project as a student intern to complete requirements for her bachelor of science degree.

Project Director:

Patricia Lockamy - Mrs. Lockamy is the North Carolina Interpretive Specialist for the Blue Ridge Parkway, where she directs education, programming, and exhibits for the North Carolina side of the park. She also serves on the Education Committee of the Appalachian Consortium.

Project Coordinators:

Dr. Roberta Herrin - Dr. Herrin is an Associate Professor of English at East Tennessee State University. An active member of the Appalachian Consortium for many years, she previously served as Chairman of the Education Committee.

Phyllis Honeycutt - Mrs. Honeycutt served as the curriculum coordinator as well as an instructor for An Appalachian Curriculum. She is also an active member of the Education Committee of the Appalachian Consortium.

TABLE OF CONTENTS

I. The Blue Ridge Parkway 6

Julian Price Memorial Park ..7

Eager Beaver 8-9
From Marshes To Meadows 10
Julian Price Word Puzzle............11-12
Beaver Poetry...................13-14
Nature Walk 15-17
Beaver Adaptations.................18
Julian Price Trip Recorder 19
The Model Beaver 20-21
Beaver Habitat.................22-23
Boone Fork Trail 24-25

Linville Falls 26

Water Collection At Linville Falls 27
Transpiration 28
Life At Linville Falls 29
Linville Falls Field Studies 30-31
Water Quality 32
Disguise A Caddisfly 33
Leprechaun vs. Dinosaur 34-35
Glossary 36
Matching 37
The ABCs Go... 38
Keying Out Leaves 39-40
A Walk In The Woods..................41

How's The Water Up There? 42
North Carolina Mapping Exercises ..43-48

II. Roan Mountain And The Appalachian Trail 49

Mapping The Appalachian Trail 50-52
Extra, Extra! Read All About It! 53-56
Roan: A Mountain Of Opportunity 57-59
Roan Word Search...................60-61
Scavenger Hunt Or Bingo..........62-63
Survival At Its Best 64
Environmental Management 65-68
Appalachian Trail Patch Design 69-70

III. Grandfather Mountain 71

Weather On Grandfather Mountain 72
Issues At Grandfather Mountain 73
Scavenger Hunt 74-78
Animals At Grandfather Mountain ..79-81
Plant Hunt 82
Animal Walk....................83
Food Web........................84
The Wildflower Coloring Book..85-91
Animal Puppets 92-96
Grandfather Mountain Wildlife Habitat............................97
Grandfather Mountain Crossword Puzzle 98-99

Museum Scavenger Hunt II ..100-102
Habitats on Grandfather Mountain 103-105
From One Teacher To Another 106
History Of Grandfather Mountain 107
My Grandfather Mountain Plant ..108
Wildflower Quilt 109
Suggested Group Activity Schedule 110
Grandfather Mountain Weather Station 111
Grandfather Mountain Information............112
Chaperone Evaluation...................113

IV. Mount Mitchell ..114

Dr. Elisha Mitchell.......................115
History of Mount Mitchell And The Black Mountains 116-117
Air Pollution Detective..................118
Climb Every Mountain 119-122
Mount Mitchell Word Search 123-124
Man And Nature..........................125
A Quilt Is The Quill 126
Field Trip Forms...................127-129

BLUE RIDGE PARKWAY

The Blue Ridge Parkway is known today as perhaps the greatest scenic highway in the world. Indeed, it was designed to meet this expectation over 60 years ago. It extends 469 miles along the crests of the Southern Appalachians and links two national parks — Shenandoah and Great Smoky Mountains. Along the way, it meanders through some of the most significant cultural and natural resources in North Carolina and Virginia. The Parkway provides seemingly endless but breathtaking views of parallel mountain ranges, scattered hills, and mountain farms.

Wildlife is abundant along the Parkway. Your students may be delighted to observe deer, bear, wild turkey, or bobcats. They may enjoy bird watching - like the hawk migrations in the spring and fall or the high elevation species such as the winter wren. Perhaps they will observe a groundhog as it sits erect along the roadside or enjoy a glimpse of a fox or opossum. They are sure to note signs of wildlife all around.

History is rich in this national park. The stories of independent mountain people are told at many overlooks along the way. There are log cabins, working farms, a mountain mansion and a grist mill. All walks of historical mountain life leave some type of tale to tell along the Parkway. In some areas, students may even observe authentic Appalachian handicraft in production.

Wherever you go along the Parkway, you will find resources to match your curriculum. Recreation areas, varying in size from several hundred to several thousand acres, are wilderness gems for those who enjoy the out-of-doors. Cultural resources are abundant. Most developed areas include picnic facilities, restrooms, water fountains and hiking trails. The Parkway offers an ideal spot for a field trip for any age group.

Be sure to be prepared for cool weather and unexpected changes in the weather. As in many mountain areas, students will need good walking shoes, plenty of food and water, and a warm jacket.

The activities that follow reflect but a sample of what you can do along the Blue Ridge Parkway with your class. We hope that you will adapt all of the activities in this book to various Parkway sites — or perhaps create a few activities of your own. For further information about the Blue Ridge Parkway call (704) 298-0398.

JULIAN PRICE MEMORIAL PARK

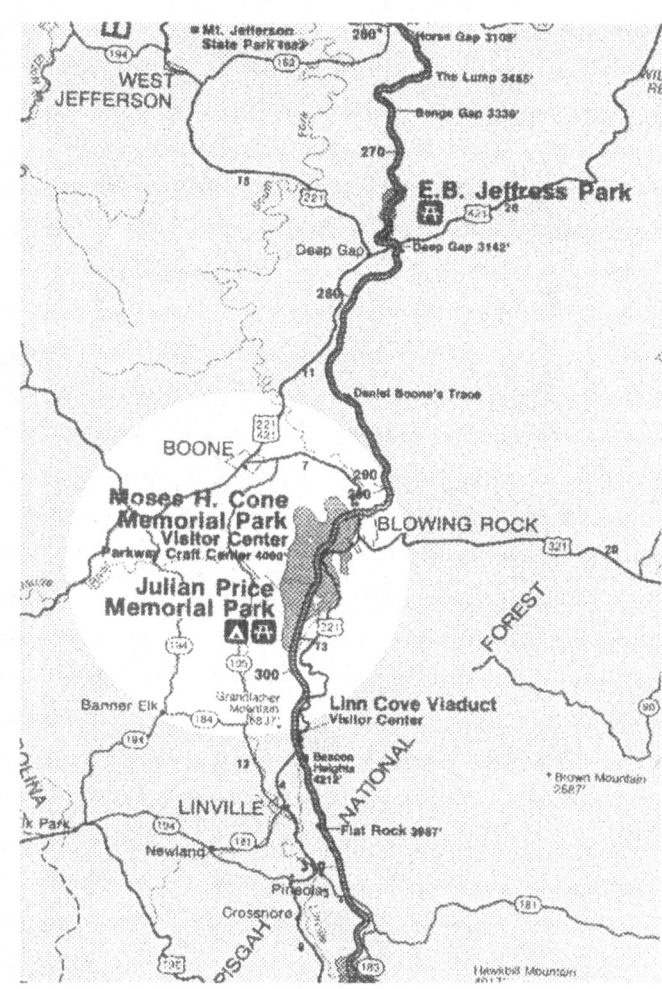

Julian Price Memorial Park is not only one of the most scenic areas along the Blue Ridge Parkway, but also one of the more diverse. The variety of resources available here make it an appealing site for any class field trip. The area offers a large picnic area, campground, hiking trails, lakes, ponds, and streams, restrooms and seasonal boat rentals. The teachers in this project especially recommend the Julian Price Picnic Area, which harbors a Natural Heritage Area and visible beaver activity along Boone Fork Creek. The trail along Boone Fork is wide, flat, and accessible directly in the picnic area. Restrooms are presently available from May through October. For detailed information, call the Blue Ridge Parkway Bluffs District Office at Sandy Flats (704) 295-7591.

The Julian Price area is also adjacent to the Moses H. Cone Memorial Park on the Blue Ridge Parkway. Here, students may gain insight into some of North Carolina's finest cultural heritage as they view the textile giant Moses Cone's mansion, which he named Flat Top Manor. The manor, now known as the Parkway Craft Center, is operated by the Southern Highlands Handicraft Guild. Authentic mountain handicraft such as pottery, hooked rugs, basketry, furniture, and hand woven materials are on sale or exhibit. Often, various skilled handicraft artists demonstrate their particular arts at the center.

The activities that follow were designed for field trips to the Julian Price Picnic Area. However, many of the activities for Linville Falls, Mt. Mitchell, and Roan Mountain would also work here. The open setting and variety of resources at Julian Price Park lend themselves to a multitude of curricula. We hope that you will find the following activities useful and that they will inspire you to design a few of your own.

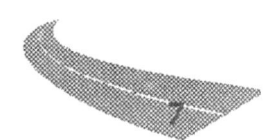

EAGER BEAVER

GOAL:
Using the beaver as an example, the learner will be aware of the relationship between the history of a region and its location, natural setting, natural resources and natural changes. Identify ways people affect the environment.

STATE OBJECTIVES:
NORTH CAROLINA:
SOCIAL STUDIES:
> The learner will evaluate ways the people of North Carolina use, modify and adapt to their physical environment.

5.3: Analyze causes and consequences of the misuse of the environment and propose alternatives.

5.3.2: Give an example of the misuse of the environment, trace its causes and construct a timeline or use other graphic organizers to exhibit these causes.

5.3.3: Given an environmental problem, predict the short-term and long-term consequences and propose alternatives.

INTRODUCTION:
The Blue Ridge Parkway, part of the National Park System, is committed to restoration and preservation of plant and animal wildlife. Wildlife management includes many different tasks, including the management of native species which were once lost but are now returning to the area.

The beaver was once master of the forest of the Southern Appalachians. As a keystone species, the beaver creates its own environment, forcing other species to adapt. Freshwater wetlands, such as bogs, are just one possible consequence of beaver territory.

The beaver is well adapted to its aquatic environment, allowing it to survive and thrive as long as its primary predator, man, allows. Beavers disappeared quickly after being discovered in the Appalachian Mountains. Hunted for its fur, killed for being a nuisance, and run off by encroaching settlers, the beaver has now reappeared along the Blue Ridge Parkway. Wildlife management techniques are again challenged by this eager aquatic mammal.

PRE-SITE ACTIVITIES:
1. Research the beaver and its unique adaptations to aquatic life.

2. Research the beaver fur trading business. Display beaver trapping areas of the U.S. on a map and develop a beaver fur store showing the uses of beaver in the late colonial era and/or early pioneer settlements.

MATERIALS:
Reference resources
Sketch pad/drawing materials
Camera (optional)
Note pad

EAGER BEAVER

ON-SITE ACTIVITIES:

1. Beaver dams at Julian Price Park are primarily constructed from a combination of sticks, leaves and mud. Observe and discuss the pros and cons of this type of construction. What skills would the beaver need to make a dam? What have been the consequences of their dams (ponds, flooding, bogs, etc.)?

2. Discuss the return of the beaver to the Blue Ridge Parkway region. When did the beaver disappear? When did it return? What positive and negative consequences have occurred since its return?

3. Beavers are crepuscular animals (active at twilight and dawn) so visitors don't usually see them. Be a beaver detective and list clues that will prove the existence of beavers at Julian Price Park. Look for tracks, evidence of beaver gnawing, dams, etc. Make sketches or map the location of your clues. What might these clues tell you about the beaver population? What is the range of beaver territory?

4. Make a list of other mammals, birds, insects, amphibians and reptiles that share the beaver's environment. Diagram the layers (levels) of each one's place in the habitat. How does this affect the food chain? How are different resources used by each type of animal?

5. As you observe the environment, notice the plant life. Many "grassy" plants near water habitats are actually sedges or rushes. Use the simple rhyme to classify the "grasses" around the bog. What geometric shapes would describe the sedge blade and the rush stem?

> SEDGES HAVE EDGES
> RUSHES ARE ROUND
> GRASSES ARE FLAT
> WHEREVER THEY ARE FOUND.

POST-SITE ACTIVITIES:

1. Make a timeline of mammal disappearance and reappearance along the Blue Ridge Parkway. A good resource is *A Naturalist's Blue Ridge Parkway* by David T. Catlin (pages 140-161).

2. Make a model, diorama or poster of a beaver dam, lodge or habitat. Explain the unique features. This could be a culmination of the research done prior to the visit.

3. Have a dam-building contest. Have individuals or groups try to make a stick dam and test if it will hold water back.

4. Write a poem or word description about the beaver.
    - B   Busy
    - E   Economic
    - A   Aquatic
    - V   Vegetarian
    - E   Environmental
    - R   Reintroduce

FROM MARSHES TO MEADOW

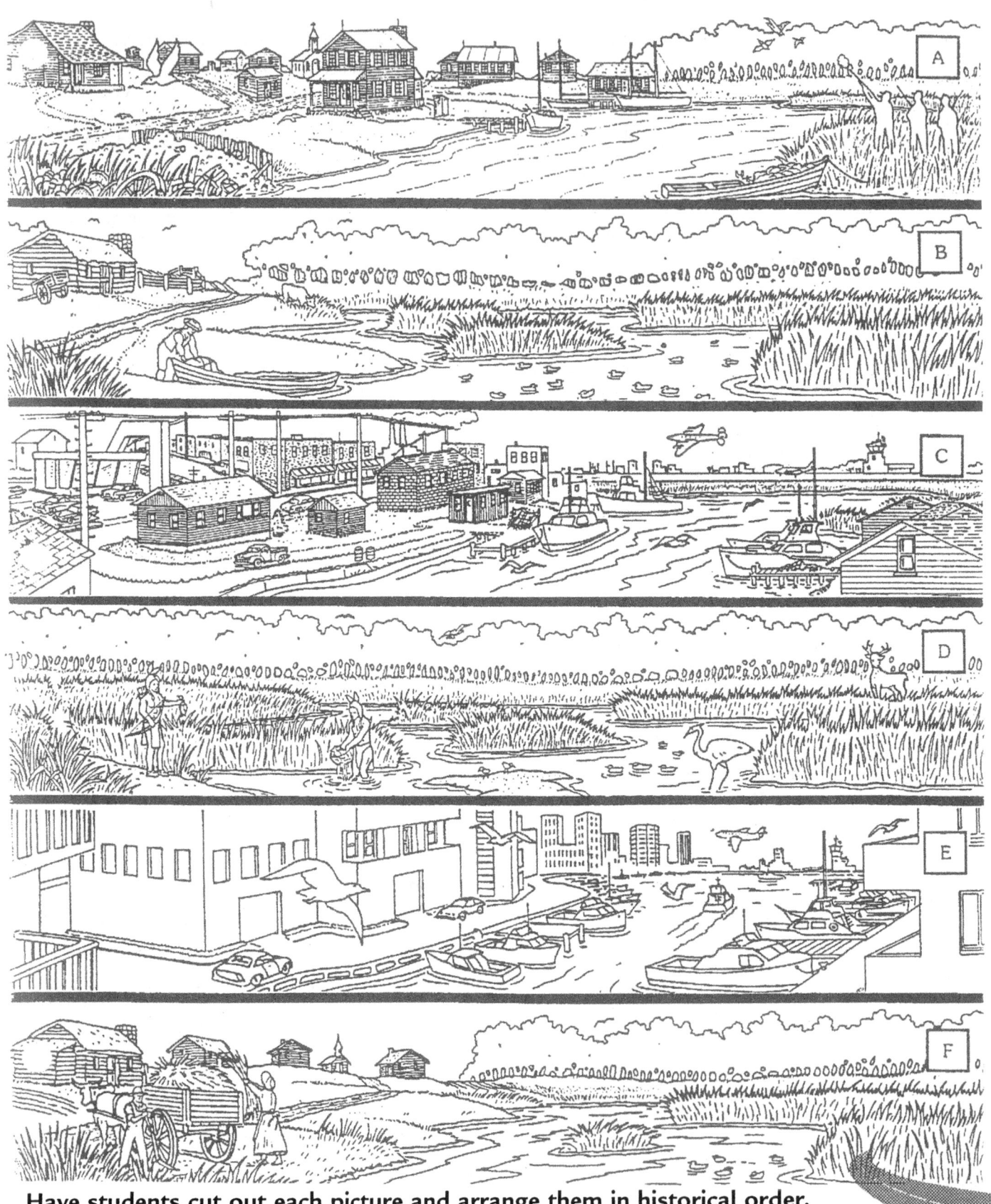

Have students cut out each picture and arrange them in historical order.

Taken from Ranger Rick Nature scope, "Wading Into Wetlands"

JULIAN PRICE WORD PUZZLE

```
J D B L U E R I D G E P A R K W A Y V M
E A X S L C E L S E D I M E N T X C B L
Z W W A I A B M Q P D O H F C A L Q X Y
S H S U R K T D G H N A I L U K Y I N P
I C S T F E C N F Y K P M J T Y A H Y Z
W R H K B Y A A K Y T R M I L E P O S T
D E I E O Q M L L M C C V L C P B N U X
N P R Y O I P T N R W Z J I L G H C T D
J U A S N L G E X M R M R B W O B L I T
S S H T E E R W W C Z P D I X I D R R W
X C T O F O O E T H N G Y S E R X G T A
W U M N O K U Y V A K B J E H G U V E O
O L G E R V N I I A D A Y D I G U T D Z
G A A S K I D L S Y E V G G V K T W J A
F R W P Y O U K P X D B J E C X Z D C F
D W B E Q J N W A B O G U S D K H E X G
Y E U C K Y T I N U M M O C C K B P N W
X K Z I Z T D W J D E G G O L R E T A W
Z B Y E T F D A E J G G O B E U T U U C
X C M S R T J N X A A D A P T A T I O N
```

WORD LIST

ADAPTATION	BEAVER	BLUERIDGEPARKWAY
BOG	BOONEFORK	CAMPGROUND
COMMUNITY	CREPUSCULAR	DAM
DETRITUS	EARTHEN	JULIANPRICE
KEYSTONESPECIES	LODGE	MILEPOST
RUSH	SEDGES	SEDIMENT
WATERLOGGED	WETLAND	

_____   _____   _____   _____   _____
_____   _____   _____   _____   _____
_____   _____   _____   _____   _____

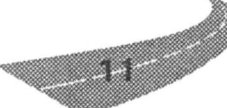

JULIAN PRICE WORD PUZZLE ANSWERS

```
. . B L U E R I D G E P A R K W A Y . .
. . . . . . E . S E D I M E N T . . . .
. . . . A . . . D . . . . . . . . . . .
. H S U R . . D . . . A . . . . . . . .
. C . T . . C N . . . M . . . . . . . .
. R H K B . A A . . . M I L E P O S T .
. E . E O . M L . . . . . C . . . U . .
N P . Y O . P T . . . . I L . . . T . .
. U . S N . G E . . . . R . . O . . I .
. S . T E . R W . . . P . . . D . R . .
. C . O F . O E . . N . . S . . . G T .
. U . N O . U . V A . . . E . . . . E .
. L . E R . N . I A . . . D . . . . D .
. A . S K . D L . . E . . G . . . . . .
. R . P . U . . B E . . . . . . . . . .
. . . E . J . . . . . . S . . . . . . .
. . . C . Y T I N U M M O C . . . . . .
. . . I . . . . D E G G O L R E T A W .
. . . E . . . . . . G O B . . . . . . .
. . . S . . . . . A D A P T A T I O N .
```

WORDLIST

ADAPTATION	BEAVER	BLUERIDGEPARKWAY
BOG	BOONEFORK	CAMPGROUND
COMMMMUNITY	CREPUSCULAR	DAM
DETRITUS	EARTHEN	JULIANPRICE
KEYSTONESPECIES	LODGE	MILEPOST
RUSH	SEDGES	SEDIMENT
WATERLOGGED	WETLAND	

BEAVER POETRY

GOAL:
The learner will develop descriptive skills by creating a diamond-shaped poem using information about beavers.

STATE OBJECTIVES:
NORTH CAROLINA:
LANGUAGE ARTS:
2: The learner will use language for the acquisition, interpretation, and application of information.

INTRODUCTION
1. Beavers travel through water like a swift bullet.
2. Beavers have flaps on their nose that close when they go underwater.
3. Beavers have clear eyelids to see underwater.
4. Beavers have chisel-like teeth that can cut a three-inch tree in five minutes.
5. Flaps come down over the beaver's teeth so they can chew underwater.
6. Beavers are very adept with their hands and fingers. Their footprints look like hands.
7. Beavers are very clumsy out of water. They use their paddle-like tails to give them balance.
8. A beaver colony consists of six to eight beavers.

ACTIVITY:
Using information about beavers learned at Julian Price Park, have students write simple diamond-shaped poems. This simplified form has seven lines. The form and a sample poem are shown below. You may want to collaborate on a few group poems to help students become comfortable with the form.

MATERIALS:
Information fact sheet about beavers
Beaver diamond-shaped poem activity sheet
Reference books
Pencils
Crayons
Markers

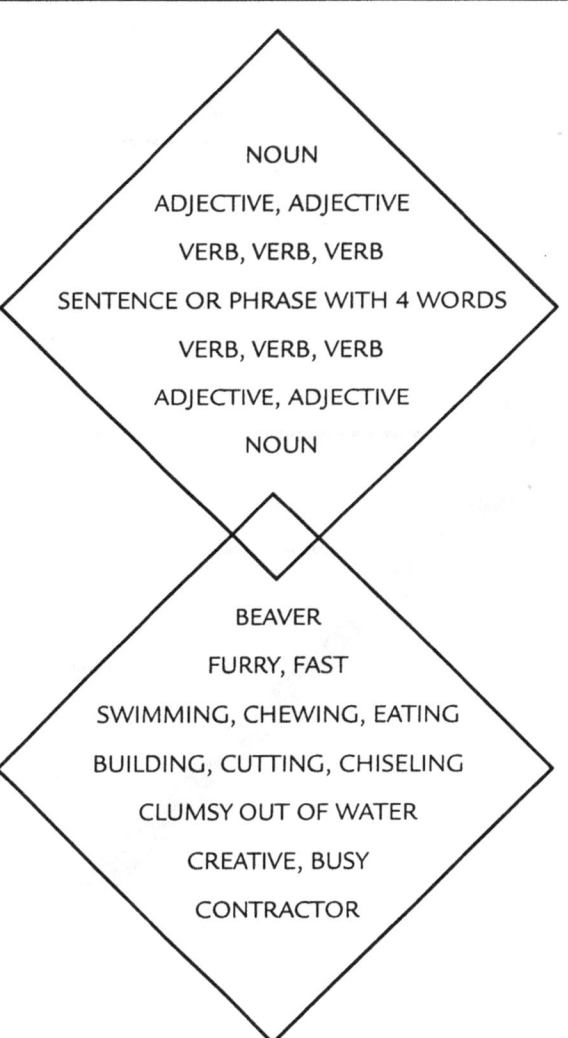

BEAVER POETRY

By:

NATURE WALK

GOAL:
The learner will identify wetlands and understand their importance. Students will discuss the beaver's role as a wetland contributor as well as some basic adaptations.

STATE OBJECTIVE:

NORTH CAROLINA:

2.4: Know that animals adapt to their environment.
2.7: Know that animals are interdependent.
6.1: Collect, organize and display data from surveys, research and classroom experiments.

TENNESSEE:

Recognize the differences among animals.
Realize how individuals impact the environment.

INTRODUCTION:

WETLANDS:

All wetlands are made of water. However, all bodies of water (ponds, lakes, rivers, creeks, etc.) are not classified as wetlands. A wetland is an area that has soggy soil or is often covered with water. These areas support plant and animal life unique only to a wetland. For this reason, wetlands are valuable and add another link among wildlife, water, land and people. It is important to protect wetlands so the plant and animal life will continue to grow and live.

A big contributor to the formation of wetlands is the beaver. An example of its work is seen at Julian Price Park. When a beaver builds its dam, the water often floods the surrounding area, turning it into a marsh or swampland.

Marshes and swamplands are two of the three types of freshwater wetlands. The types of freshwater wetlands are:

1. Marshes make up about 90% of wetlands. The vegetation that grows there is the trademark of a marsh. Some common forms of vegetation are grasses, sedges, rushes, cattails, and water lilies. It has been said that marshes are close to being the most efficient habitats on Earth. They provide food, shelter and water.

2. Bogs are freshwater wetlands that usually consist of peat, which is rich organic material made of decaying plant material. Layers of peat can be 40 feet thick. Peat contains acid and decays matter very slowly. Material, from prehistoric time to the present, that is buried in it often is well preserved.

3. Swamps are usually overtaken by shrubs and trees. The amount of water in a swamp can vary from a small amount to several feet deep. Swamps can support a variety of animal life. Animals such as alligators, panthers and raccoons can live in a swamp.

BEAVERS:

The beaver is adapted to living in water. It has flaps to cover its ears and mouths and an extra pair of clear eyelids to swim in the water. A beaver builds a dam to create a water environment in which to live. Until a pond is formed, it lives in the sides of riverbanks, and the entrance to its home is underwater to deter predators.

Once the pond is the size it likes, the beaver builds its lodge in the middle. The flooding causes nearby trees to collapse, and fish, duck and amphibians find a new home. Predators are then attracted to the area by the possibilities of prey.

Beavers are important along the Blue Ridge Parkway because they are the only aquatic mammal living there. Beavers became extinct in North Carolina because of the beaver fur trade in the settler's time, but it was reintroduced to the area.

NATURE WALK

PRE-SITE ACTIVITIES:

1. Complete the matching/defining worksheet.

2. List different kinds of animals found in a wetland.

3. Research the beaver. Find other adaptations it has and how it lives.

ON-SITE ACTIVITIES:

1. Have students describe the beaver habitat: such as plants, animals, the way it looks, water level, how soggy the ground is.

2. What do we mean by habitat?

3. Point out other habitats created due to the environment the beaver created.

4. Could the habitat change? How? What do you think would happen then?

5. Set aside time for student to do solo work. Make sure students spread out. Have them write down everything they see, hear, smell or feel. After a specified time, have them share their list with the class. Make a master list of all the things they found.

POST-SITE ACTIVITIES:

1. Take the master list and make a wetland model from it. This can be as big as a wall mural or as small as individual pictures.

MATERIALS:

Construction paper
Scissors
Glue
Crayons/markers
Tape/stapler
Cardboard, egg cartons

ON-SITE GAME: Bulldozer

DIRECTIONS:

Pick two opposite sides of the playing field as boundaries. Then pick two or three people to be the bulldozers. The bulldozers stand in the middle of the playing field. Everyone else are wildlife standing along one of the boundary lines.

Tell the bulldozers to turn around because you are going to pick several beavers. The bulldozers cannot know who the beavers are because the beavers are the only ones who can save the wildlife and make the bulldozers' job harder. Once the beavers are selected, the bulldozers can turn around.

The bulldozers yell, "Give me some wildlife!" Everyone has to run and try to make it to the other boundary without being tagged by the bulldozers.

If the wildlife get tagged, they have to stand in that spot like a tree until a beaver saves them. Beavers can save wildlife by running by them and touching their feet. Beavers can only do this on the next run back to the boundary.

If a beaver gets tagged, it cannot be saved by other beavers. It has to lay in the spot looking like a road kill. Everyone keeps running back and forth (on the bulldozers' cues) until all are tagged by the bulldozers.

NATURE WALK

WETLAND WORKSHEET

MATCHING:

1. ___ Freshwater wetland that consists of peat.

2. ___ An animal adapted for living in water.

3. ___ Acidic organic material.

4. ___ An area often covered with water.

5. ___ It supports a variety of animal life.

6. ___ The most efficient habitat on Earth.

A) Wetland
B) Marsh
C) Bog
D) Peat
E) Swamp
F) Beaver

Answer: 1-C, 2-F, 3-D, 4-A, 5-E, 6-B

QUESTIONS:

1. How does a beaver make a wetland?

2. Why are wetlands valuable to the environment?

3. What kind of vegetation grows in a marsh?

4. Why are things well-preserved in a bog?

5. What kind of animal life can a swamp support?

6. Where do beavers live before they build a lodge?

7. Why is the beaver important on the Blue Ridge Parkway?

REFERENCES

Miller, Arthur P. and Marjourie, L. *Park Ranger Guide to Rivers and Lakes*. Stackpole Books, 1991.

National Park Service. National Parks and Conservation Association. *Biological Diversity Curriculum: Make a World of Difference*. National Parks and Conservation Association. Minnesota Environmental Ed. Board, 1990.

National Wildlife Federation. *Ranger Rick's Nature Scope: Wading into Wetlands*, 1992.

BEAVER ADAPTATIONS

GOAL:
The learner will construct an understanding of science concepts through analyzing systems. The learner will demonstrate an understanding and use of graphing.

STATE OBJECTIVES:

NORTH CAROLINA:

SCIENCE
- 5.2: Investigate animals and their behaviors within natural environments
- 5.2.1: Compare and contrast various adaptations of different animal groups to their environment

MATH
- 6.1: Collect, organize and display data from classroom experiments
- 6.2: Formulate questions and interpret information from charts, tables, and graphs

TENNESSEE:

SCIENCE:
- Recognize the differences among animals
- Realize how individuals impact the environment

MATH:
- Use information from tables, charts and graphs to solve problems

PRE-SITE ACTIVITY:
Use these activities in conjunction with a unit of study on animals or, specifically, beavers. Students will research animals and compare similarities of animal groups by sharing their projects. Include the concept of animal adaptation.

ON-SITE ACTIVITY:

1. Take a "Beaver Walk" (arrange through the Blue Ridge Parkway). Have students note in notebooks/sketch pads all signs of beavers, such as tree fellings, lodges and dams.

2. As a class, brainstorm beaver adaptations. Include:
   · Hands that are human-like
   · Long fingers for manipulation
   · Webbed feet for swimming
   · Tail for balance and swimming
   · Chiseled, sharp teeth for felling trees
   · Flap behind teeth and nose for protection underwater

3. Create a Venn diagram to depict similarities and differences between beavers and human adaptations. Use two hoops to create the Venn diagram. List adaptations separately on index cards. Students then place cards on the Venn diagram, prompting discussion. The cards can be from students during the brainstorming session or noted in advance. Include the following:

Webbed feet	Toes
Tail	Hands
Flap behind teeth/nose	Feet
Chiseled Teeth	Hair

JULIAN PRICE TRIP RECORDER

1. Destination: _____
2. Departure time: _____
3. Present temperature/weather conditions: _____
4. Beginning mileage: _____
5. Ending mileage: _____
6. How far? _____
7. Arrival time: _____
8. Temperature/weather conditions at destination: _____
9. Elevation: _____
10. Watershed? _____

SKETCHES AND NOTES

THE MODEL BEAVER

GOAL:
The goal of this lesson is to educate students about wildlife that lives in mountain streams, such as in Julian Price Park.

OBJECTIVE:
The learner will understand the physical characteristics of beavers and how they live. Students will build a model of the animal's habitat and place it on a model of human habitat. Students will use problem-solving skills to think of ways man and animals can live together. Teachers will give background information and lead the discussion.

STRANDS:
Science and Art

STATE OBJECTIVES:
NORTH CAROLINA:
- 2: The learner will have a general knowledge of animals.
- 2.4: Know that animals are adapted to their environment.
- 2.7.5: Discuss how humans must care for the environment to insure that animals remain healthy and species survive.

TENNESSEE:
- 35401: Understanding the effects of environmental change to inhabitants.
- 354P1: Understand the basic concept of habitat and how habitats can be preserved.

BACKGROUND INFORMATION:
The North American beaver is an intelligent animal, according to Indian folklore. It is a hard worker, with physical characteristics that allow it to build a lodge in one day. The North American beaver weighs 35 to 40 pounds, and its body is about two feet in length. The tail is usually about one-third as long as its body, or about 10 inches.

The beaver has reddish-brown outer fur and dark-brown under fur. The fur protects the beaver and keeps it warm and dry. The beaver has a round body, strong head and powerful jaws and teeth for chiseling trees. The beaver's two teeth have sharp edges that become worn, but these teeth continue to grow throughout the beaver's life.

The beaver has flaps inside its ears and a mouth that closes when it swims. The beaver has two eyelids — one is a clear lid that closes when underwater. The beaver's front feet have joints like human hands, allowing the beaver to construct its lodge precisely. The beaver's back feet are webbed for swimming, and its tail is broad, flat and covered with scales. The beaver uses its tail as a rudder for swimming and to sit up. The beaver is a graceful swimmer and can stay underwater for 20 minutes. The beaver also uses its tail to warn others by slapping it on the surface of the water.

The beaver lives in a colony of six to eight beavers. A beaver's life begins as a kit, which are born in litters of two to six beavers. The kits live with their mothers for three years and then find a mate and build a lodge of their own.

The beaver's lodge, or home, is constructed in the ground with an opening to the water. The lodge has two rooms- a "mud" or work room and a "living" room where they rest. The lodges are made of mud and sticks from poplar, aspen, willow and birch trees, and the beaver eats bark from these trees. The beaver works at night, during early sunrise or during late sunset. The beaver stores food and spends the winter resting in his lodge.

The beaver is a "keystone" species, just like humans, meaning they manipulate their environment to suit their needs.

THE MODEL BEAVER

PRE-SITE ACTIVITIES:
1. Research the beaver, his dam and lodge. Make lists of other rodent families.

2. What role does the beaver play in natural resources and wildlife? What role did the beaver have during the fur trade height?

ACTIVITIES:
Construct a model of a 20-acre habitat for people and beavers.

Use butcher paper to draw land and streams. Cut trees out of colored paper and make a forest on some of the property. Have students remove trees as they need for constructing their houses.

Talk about the fact that beavers live there and the people will be moving in on the beavers. What will happen to the beavers?

Have students build a house out of a box. Discuss what is happening to the animal habitat as the activity continues. Visit Julian Price Park and see the animal habitat. Ask students to identify the current problems for man and the beaver. Have students think of ways to improve the situation, such as designating wildlife areas like Julian Price Park.

POST-SITE ACTIVITIES:
1. Draw a picture of a beaver's lodge and dam or construct a model diorama out of papier-mâché.

2. Write a story. Pretend you are a beaver and discuss your problems and what you can do to make your life better.

BEAVER HABITAT

GOAL:
To look at the ways that management of our animal resources ensures endangered or threatened species will survive.

STATE OBJECTIVE:
NORTH CAROLINA:
2.7.5: Discuss how humans must care for the environment to ensure that animals remain healthy and survive

TENNESSEE:
To realize how individuals effect the environment

BACKGROUND INFORMATION:
The reintroduction of endangered and threatened animals is controversial. (An example is the current controversy over the reintroduction of the Red Wolf to the Smokies.) The reintroduction of the beaver to this area has caused some conflict also. The beaver has done so well in its habitat that it has conflicted with its neighbors over land. This conflict occurs when the beavers dam streams, and the subsequent flooding causes problems for man.

PRE-SITE ACTIVITIES:
1. Compare the goals and values of those who want to protect the beaver with those who want to remove the beaver.

2. Beavers require considerable land and water resources that could be used for other purposes. Discuss these uses and debate which is best.

3. Collect news articles and information about beavers and discuss the information in class.

4. Debate the issue of man versus the beaver over the right to use the land.

DEBATE: SHOULD ANIMALS BE PROTECTED?

SHOULD		SHOULD NOT
They are natural resources.	vs.	They provide resources.
They can become endangered.	vs.	They get in man's way.
Animals should be protected.	vs.	Animals shouldn't be protected.

DIRECTIONS: This is a basic outline for a simple debate. The students will need to do research to have sufficient information for the debate. They may pick sides or the teacher may assign sides.

OTHER POSSIBLE TOPICS:

1. The effect of the fur trade on animal populations.

2. The effect the decline in animal populations had on Native Americans.

3. The fur trade's affect on the settlement of remote areas?

ON-SITE ACTIVITY:
As the students visit the beaver habitat, have them make drawings of their observations (the type of dams, evidence of conflict with man and the environment, etc.) Were the dams and surroundings what the students expected? If not, what was different?

Continued on following page.

BEAVER HABITAT

POST-SITE ACTIVITIES:
BEAVER HABITAT

Study the drawing below. Is this the type of beaver habitat you observed?
How do you account for differences you observed?
Look carefully at the Beaver lodge.
What kind of builder do you think the beaver is?
What special adaptations would it needs?

_____
_____
_____
_____
_____
_____
_____
_____
_____
_____

BOONE FORK TRAIL

GOAL:
To educate students about beavers and their adaptation.

STATE OBJECTIVES:
NORTH CAROLINA:

SCIENCE: All

LANGUAGE ARTS: All

SOCIAL STUDIES:

5.3: Analyze causes and consequences of the misuse of the physical environment and propose alternatives.

5.3.2: Give an example of the misuse of the environment, trace its causes and construct a timeline or use other graphic organizers to exhibit these causes.

5.3.3: Given an environment problem, predict the short-term and long-term consequences if nothing were done and propose alternatives to doing nothing.

MATH: All

MUSIC/DRAMA: Role play an endangered species.

HEALTH: Actions produce consequences.

TENNESSEE:

SCIENCE: All

SOCIAL STUDIES: All

PRE-SITE ACTIVITIES:
1. Have students research beavers using books.

2. Have students design and draw their interpretation of a beaver, its home and its structures.

3. Through role play, have students work together as individuals or groups to show how the beaver works to survive.

MATERIALS:
Art paper (manilla is best)
Pencils
Crayons
Chalk
Markers
Colored pencils
Index cards to label groups/individuals
Rope to mark off space for role-play
Resources: books on beavers

BOONE FORK TRAIL

ON-SITE ACTIVITIES:

1. Have students sketch field drawings of beavers (should they be so lucky to see one), their dens, their dams and the remains of trees they have used.

2. Have students take pictures of these areas and label.

3. Have students approximate the length of the beaver, body and tail from a safe distance.

MATERIALS:

Individual field journals
Tape measure
Cameras (automatic processing is best)
Film
Plastic sandwich baggies (to store photos)
Permanent markers
Resources: books on photography and beaver mount (possibly available on-site)

POST-SITE ACTIVITIES:

1. Create a life-size papier-mâché beaver (use photos, field journals, and measurements as a resource).

2. Divide the class into the same groups or by individuals and have them work together as a beaver colony to build dens, dams, etc.

3. Develop and write a story about the beaver or the park visit, either fact or fiction. Make it into a report with photos.

MATERIALS:

Cartons of wheat paste
Newspaper
Chicken wire
Floral wire (for holding it together)
Paints
Markers
Small photo albums or photo protectors
Report Covers
Pencils
Resources: Papier-mâché art guide

LINVILLE FALLS

Blue Ridge Parkway Milepost 316

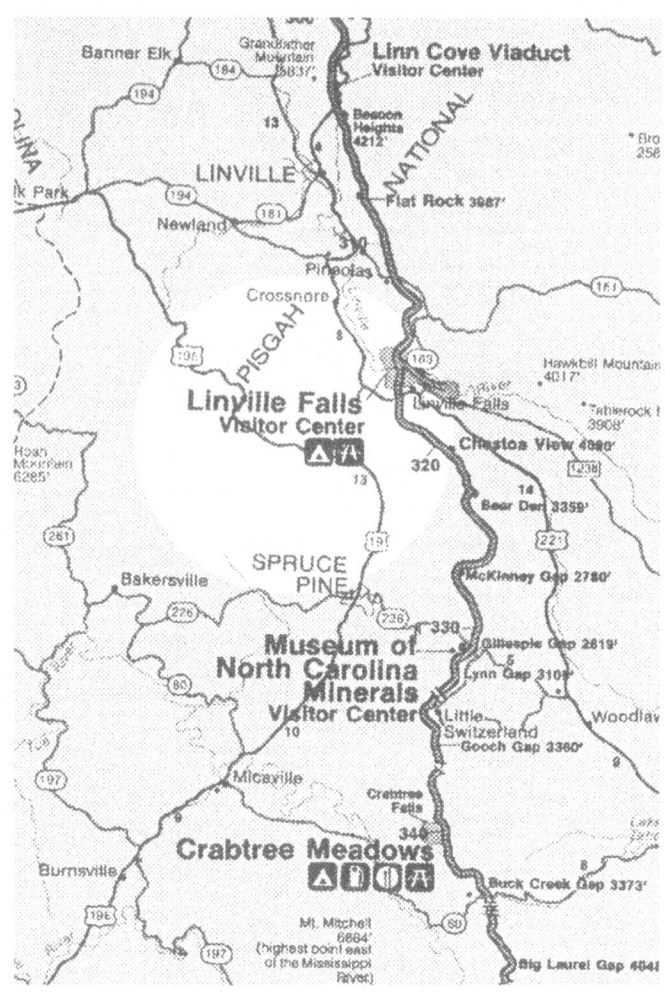

Linville Falls has always been one of the most popular stops along the Blue Ridge Parkway. Located close to the town of Linville Falls, North Carolina, the area features spectacular views of the scenic falls through Linville Gorge. In addition to the falls, your class may enjoy the more quiet aquatic areas of Duggers Creek and the Linville River or perhaps the picnic area, visitor center, campground, hiking trails and restrooms. Linville Falls is accessible by traveling Route 221 to the Blue Ridge Parkway, then following the signs north to the falls area. A wide, relatively flat, one-half mile trail leads from the visitor center to the water falls.

The trail system leads first to a view of the upper falls, a relatively broad but shallow drop occurring before the water makes a second, spectacular plunge over the lower falls. The plant life along the trail, both by the riverbanks and throughout the gorge includes an abundance of rare species, virgin hemlock, and a great variety of hardwood trees and wildflowers. The stream border between the two falls is one of the few locales in the mountains where you can find the three native rhododendrons growing side by side: the rosebay, catawba, and carolina.

Most of the following activities can be accomplished with your class along the trail to the falls or in the classroom. The aquatic activities were designed for the quiet areas of the Linville River and Duggers Creek, both of which are accessible from the Linville Falls parking area. For more information about Linville Falls, call the Blue Ridge Parkway Gillespie Gap District Office at (704) 765-6082.

WATER COLLECTION AT LINVILLE FALLS

GOAL:
The students will develop an understanding of the process of transpiration. The learner will demonstrate transpiration and will calculate how much water the plant will give off in a day.

STATE OBJECTIVES:
STRAND: Science and Math

NORTH CAROLINA:

6.1: Collect, organize and display data from surveys, research and classroom experiments, including data collected over a period of time. Include data from other disciplines such as science, physical education and social studies.

4: The learner will understand and use standard units of metric and customary measure.

TENNESSEE:

MATH

·Multiply up to a four-digit number by a one-digit number.

·Solve one-step word problems involving addition, subtraction, multiplication and basic division facts.

·Measure length, weight (mass) and liquid capacity in standard or metric units.

BACKGROUND INFORMATION:
Transpiration cannot be seen just by looking at a plant. When the plant's leaf pores open to allow the carbon dioxide to come in and the oxygen to flow out, water evaporates from the leaves to keep the leaf from overheating. This process is called transpiration. Scientists estimate that an acre of corn gives off 4,000 gallons of water a day.

FIELD STUDY

As you begin your hike, select several leaves on different species of trees. Place a baggie over the leaves and close your bag.
Record the time:

Continue your walk.

Record the time you returned:

Describe the condition of the bag, then answer the following questions.

1. How long were you gone?

2. Measure the water in the bag. How much did you collect?

3. Where did the water come from?

4. If you used the leaves from more than one species of tree, which species produced the most water?

5. Find the rate of transpiration. Use the time and the amount of water produced to figure the ratio.

6. In the space below, draw and illustrate the water cycle. How are we dependent on trees?

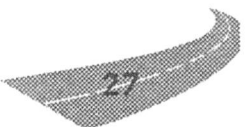

TRANSPIRATION

BACKGROUND:
Plants have a cooling effect on our environment due to "air conditioning" created by evaporation of water through the surface of the leaves. This process is called transpiration. Large quantities of water are released into the atmosphere through this process.

MATERIALS NEEDED:
Plastic ruler
Plastic baggies
Graduated cylinder
Watch

ACTIVITY:
Select several different leaves, cover with the plastic baggie, then complete the following chart.

Leaf name	Start time	Stop time	Total H_2O	Comments

LIFE AT LINVILE FALLS

Whirligig Beetle

Whirligig Larvae

Caddisfly

Caddisfly Larvae

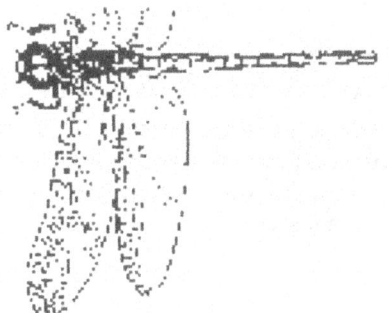

Dragonfly

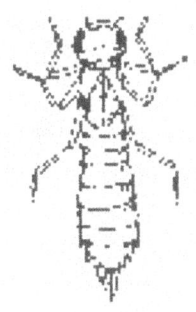

Dragonfly Nymph

Stonefly

Stonefly Nymph

Frog

Tadpole

Reference: Aquatic Project Wild

LINVILLE FALLS FIELD STUDIES

GOAL:
To study an aquatic community and understand how the members interact.

OBJECTIVES:

NORTH CAROLINA:

2.4: Know that animals are adapted to their environment

TENNESSEE:

To realize environmental problems vary from one community to another

PRE-SITE ACTIVITIES:

1. Have students study the life cycle of various aquatic insects and draw the stages of the life cycle.

2. Have students discuss how most adults react to insects. Have students list beneficial and harmful insects. Have students decide what would happen to various insects if a part of their life cycle was destroyed.

ON-SITE ACTIVITY:

Have students complete the field study on the following page. Dugger's Creek, located adjacent to the parking area at Linville Falls, is an excellent site to observe aquatic life. Photocopy the drawings of aquatic creatures on the preceding page for your students to assist in their identification of common aquatic life.

POST-SITE ACTIVITY:

Have students do a follow-up of their favorite insect. They may want to draw pictures or make a diorama to show the mini-ecosystem of the insect.

FIELD STUDY

OBJECTIVE:
A stream or pond is an excellent example of the delicate balance of its inhabitants. By careful observation and analysis, one can learn much about the interrelationship between living things and their environment.

ACTIVITY:
A. Select a pond or stream.

B. Complete a field observation.

   1. Give the location of your body of water:

   2. Record the temperature of the water: _____ °F _____ °C

      Record the time of the observation:

   3. Record the factors which would affect the water temperature, shade, depth, rate of flow, etc.

   4. Record the type of rock around the stream:

   5. Is there shading? If so, how much?

   6. Describe the amount of turbidity:

      List factors that affect the turbidity:

WORKSHEET FOR AQUATIC ANIMALS
COMPLETE THE FOLLOWING CHART:

Name	Adult/Nymph/Larva	Habitat	Behavior	Food
Caddisfly	Larva	on rock	stone house	carnivore
Dragonfly	nymph	in water	fast moving	aquatic

Comments:

WATER QUALITY

GOAL:
The learner will evaluate how people of North Carolina use, modify and adapt to the physical environment. The learner will understand and use standard units of metric and customary measure and solve problems and reason mathematically. The learner will demonstrate an understanding and use of graphing, probability and statistics. The learner will use language for the acquisition, interpretation and application of information. The learner will develop the ability to use science process skills.

STATE OBJECTIVES:
NORTH CAROLINA:
SOCIAL STUDIES:
5.2: Explain how North Carolinians use, modify or adapt to their physical environment

MATH:
4.11: Formulate and solve meaningful problems involving length, weight, time, capacity and temperature and verify reasonableness of answers
5.3: Determine whether there are sufficient data to solve problems
5.6: Solve problems by observation and/or computation using calculators and computers when appropriate
5.7: Verify and interpret results with respect to the original problem. Discuss alternate methods for solutions
5.8: Formulate engaging problems including ones from everyday situations
6.1: Collect, organize and display data from surveys, research and classroom experiments, including data collected over a period of time. Include data from other disciplines such as science and social studies.

LANGUAGE ARTS:
2.1: Identify, collect or select information and ideas
2.2: Analyze, synthesize and organize information and discover related ideas, concepts or generalizations
2.3: Apply, extend and expand on information and concepts

SCIENCE:
2.1: Demonstrate the ability to observe
2.2: Demonstrate the ability to classify
2.3: Demonstrate the ability to use numbers

BACKGROUND INFORMATION:
Discuss with students these indicators of water quality:

1. appearance
2. pH
3. smell
4. temperature
5. species living in the water (number and variety)

ON-SITE ACTIVITY:
Students will collect data and prepare a graphic organizer (use the chart below or create own) to compare water quality at Linville to other locations. Students will make predictions before collecting data and make conclusions about the research.

Discussion questions may include:

1. Is this water source a watershed?
2. What can you conclude about the number of living species in this water source?
3. How does the pH level compare at each of the collection sights?
   (Students can then graph the data.)

MATERIALS:
pH kit
Thermometer
Magnifying glass
Collection jars
Chart or notebook for recording data

Location	Prediction	Appearance	Smell	Temperature	pH	Species	Conclusion

DISGUISE A CADDISFLY

GOAL:
The learner will construct a caddisfly case using materials from nature.

OBJECTIVES:
NORTH CAROLINA:
SCIENCE 2:
·The learner will have a general knowledge of animals and insects.
·The learner will recognize that animals and insects are adapted to their environment.

INTRODUCTION:
The caddisfly is an insect that spends much of its yearlong life underwater. When caddisflies are found in streams, it is a good indication the water is of good quality. Other insects that are "good water" indicators are the mayfly and the stonefly. Trout and other fish love to eat the caddisfly so to protect itself, the larva builds a camouflaged case around its body.

ACTIVITY:
To make a caddisfly case, use a thin cardboard tube. Close the tube at one end with tape. Cover the entire tube with glue. Cover the tube with natural materials such as leaves, twigs, small rocks. Use materials that will camouflage the tube. Make the caddisfly larva using modeling clay. Put the larva inside the tube.

MATERIALS:
Thin cardboard tube
Tape
Glue
Clay
Leaves
Twigs
Small rocks

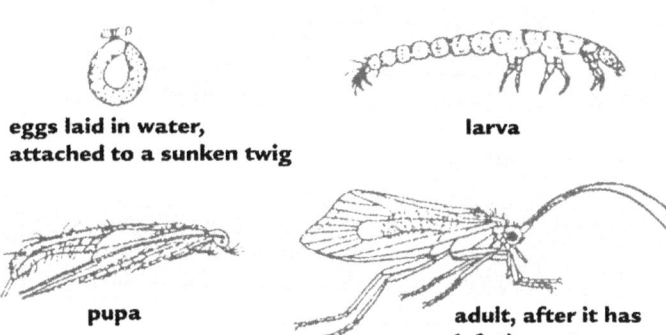

eggs laid in water, attached to a sunken twig

larva

pupa

adult, after it has left the water

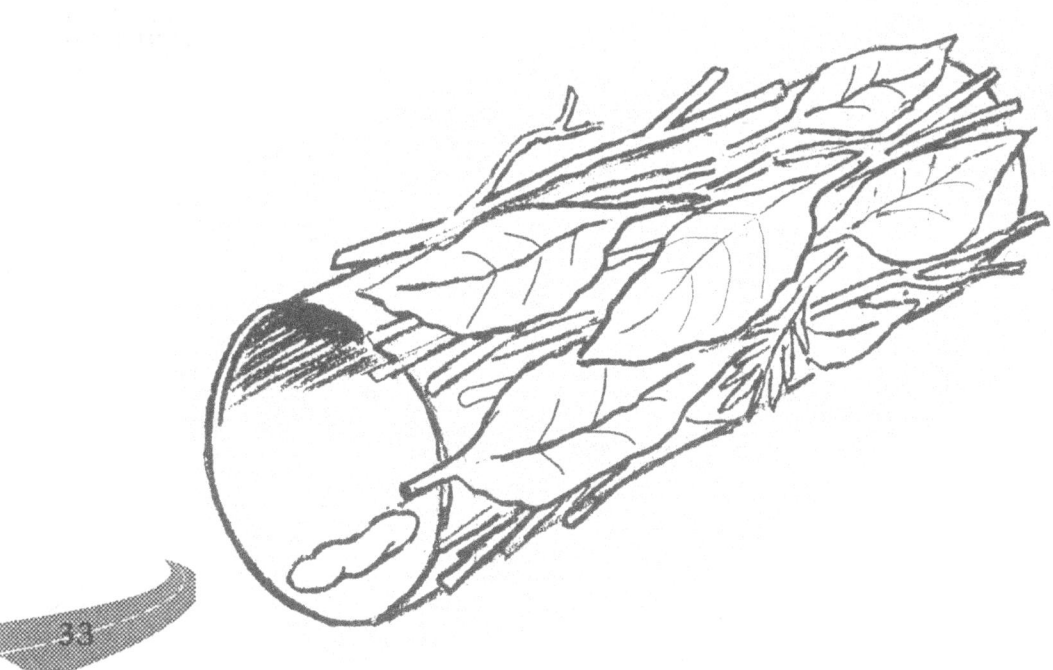

LEPRECHAUN vs. DINOSAUR

GOAL:
The learner will be aware and recognize a community's layered effect and its impact on plants and animals that share the same ecosystem.

STATEOBJECTIVES:
NORTH CAROLINA
MATH :
The learner will solve problems and reason mathematically.
6.1: Collect, organize and display data from surveys.
SCIENCE 2:
The learner will have a general knowledge of animals.
2.4: Know that plants and animals are adapted to their environment.
2.7: Know that plants and animals are interdependent.
SKILLS:
Observing, classifying, measuring, predicting, interpreting.

MATERIALS:
Measuring items — rulers, tape measures, yardsticks
Field guides to trees, plants, animals
Sketch pad with paper for rubbings
Pencils or other writing tools, coloring implements
Charts

PRE-SITE ACTIVITY:

1. Familiarize the students with field guide books on trees, wild flowers, etc.

2. Trial runs of identification processes, taxonomy may be done closer to home. *See Ranger Rick's Nature Scope "Trees are Terrific"* (pages 14 and 20-22).

3. Practice measuring tall trees in the neighborhood using the steps found in *Ranger Rick's Nature Scope "Trees are Terrific"* (page 57).

4. The height of a tree is measured from the ground to its top twig approximated to the nearest foot. Students need to stay on level ground as they measure.

   A. Hold your arm in front of you so your fist is at eye level. Have another team member measure the distance from your fist to your eye.

   B. Face the tree and hold a yardstick straight vertically so the distance from your hand to the top of the stick is the same as the distance measured in step A.

   C. Walk backward away from the tree until you can see the base of the tree by looking over your fist and the top of the tree by looking over the top of the yardstick.

   D. When you can see the tree completely by looking over the top of the yardstick and the top of your fist, another person should measure the distance between you and the tree. This distance is the approximate height of the tree.

LEPRECHAUN vs. DINOSAUR

ACTIVITY:

Divide the class into Leprechauns and Dinosaurs. The Leprechaun group will compile a list of plants and animals less than 12 inches tall or long. The Dinosaur group will compile a list of plants and animals more than 24 inches tall or long. The buffer zone of 12-24 inches is discretionary for the teacher/guide.

Encourage the children to be as specific in their lists as possible. For example, list "White Oak" rather than just "tree". Some items may be on both lists (example, White Oak tree and oak seedling, robin and robin's egg). Mushrooms and lichens may be distinguished by color, shape or other characteristics.

Each group/person may use measuring instruments such as rulers and tape measures. When actual measurement is not feasible, estimation skills should be encouraged.

Students should fill in the information on the chart as the items are found. Age can be as simple as "growing" or "full grown". It's fun to guess the age of trees by their size. Some groups may want to describe the location, focusing on the soil (moist, dry, dark, light, rocky, sandy), lighting (sunny, shady, canopy, understory), etc.

Sketches, leaf or bark rubbings or photographs may be used for accuracy and enhancement.

Teachers may want to designate the areas for the groups. Teachers may assign the collection to include as few or as many items as time and opportunity will allow. (Five to 10 items can usually be collected.)

Warn the students about handling plants and animals and discourage trampling.

Use the following headings for your chart:
    Location
    Plant/Animal
    Number found
    Distinguishing characteristics
    Measurement estimate
    Age

Upon completion of each group's compiled list, the groups should compare lists by plant or animals listed, characteristics, measurements, etc.

QUESTIONS ABOUT THE PLANTS:

1. What was the smallest plant found?
2. Largest plant found?
3. Most unusual?
4. Most colorful?
5. Most frequently found plant?
6. Least frequently found plant?

QUESTIONS ABOUT THE ANIMALS:

1. What was the smallest animal found?
2. Largest animal found?
3. Most unusual?
4. Most colorful?
5. Most frequently found animal?
6. Least frequently found animal?

Discuss the environment and habitat for the plants and animals. Why were they found at this location? What was healthy/unhealthy for them?

POST-SITE ACTIVITIES:

1. Have groups make a mural or model of their findings.
2. Have groups share information and make a plausible food chain diagram for their location.
3. Have each group/person write a story about living as a leprechaun or dinosaur in the environment they charted.

GLOSSARY

Acid Rain: A type of pollution that occurs when sulfur and nitrogen compounds in the atmosphere react with water vapor.

Adaptation: A behavior, physical feature or other characteristic that helps an animal or plant survive in its habitat.

Barometer: An instrument for measuring atmospheric pressure. Also used to measure height above sea level.

Biological Control: A natural means of controlling pests.

Bog: Poorly drained freshwater wetlands characterized by a build-up of peat.

Botany: The study of plant life, structure, growth and classification.

Canopy: Uppermost layer of most forests. Made up of branches and leaves of the tallest trees.

Climax forest: The final stage in plant succession.

Community: A group of interacting plants and animals living in the same area.

Crepuscular: An animal that is active just before twilight or just before sunrise (beaver).

Deciduous trees: Trees that lose all their leaves each year.

Decomposers: Dead material turned into useful nutrient-rich organic matter to be used by other plants to live and grow (fungi, lichens, mosses and decomposers).

Deforestation: The process of clearing forests.

Detritus: Bits of vegetation, animal remains and other organic material that form the base of food chains in wetlands and other habitats.

Ecosystem: All living things and their environments in an area of any size, linked by the flow of energy and nutrients.

Ecology: Study of relations of living things to one another and to their environment.

Edge effect: An area where two types of vegetation come together. Animals tend to concentrate in these areas because of diversity of food and shelter.

Endemic: Native or common to a region. Always present.

Exploitation: To take advantage of a resource selfishly and unethically.

Endangered species: A species in immediate danger of becoming extinct.

Evergreen trees: Trees that do not lose all of their leaves each year.

Extinct: No longer living.

Forestry: The science of managing forests.

Geology: The structure of the Earth's crust in a particular region.

Habitat: A space, area or type of environment that includes water, food and shelter that an animal needs to survive and reproduce.

Humus: Layers of soil and organic material in a forest floor, including decaying leaves, needles, etc. (litter).

Multiple use management: The practice of managing a forest for several uses (mining, camping, logging, etc.).

Niche: A special place in a community occupied by a certain organism. The role of an organism in its community or habitat.

Peat: Partially decomposed plants and other organic material that builds up in poorly-drained wetland habitats.

Percolation: Downward flow or infiltration of water through the pores or spaces of rock and soil.

Pioneer species: Plants capable of invading bare sites and living there until another plant replaces it.

Population: A group of animals or plants of the same species that live in the same area.

Raptors: Birds which are predatory (hawks, owls, eagles).

Sediment: Particles of sand, soil and minerals that are washed from the land and settle on the bottoms of wetlands and aquatic habitats.

Silviculture: The cultivation of forest and shade trees.

Stomata: Small pores in a tree's leaves and stems that open to absorb carbon dioxide and release oxygen.

Succession: The orderly, gradual and continuous replacement of one kind of plant community by another. The change in plant and animal life over time.

Threatened species: A species whose numbers are low or declining.

Transpiration: The process by which a tree loses water through stomata on its leaves and stems.

Understory: Layer formed by the crowns of smaller trees in a forest.

Watershed: An area which drains into a stream, lake, river or system of rivers. Drainage is due to the slope of ridges, causing water to flow downward (divide).

Wetlands: Areas that, at least periodically, have waterlogged soils or are covered with a relatively shallow layer of water. Bogs, freshwater and saltwater marshes, and freshwater and saltwater swamps are examples.

MATCHING

1. Watershed _____
2. Forestry _____
3. Community _____
4. Extinct _____
5. Population _____
6. Sediment _____
7. Transpiration _____
8. Stomata _____
9. Adaptation _____
10. Habitat _____
11. Bog _____
12. Succession _____
13. Peat _____
14. Deciduous _____
15. Decomposers _____
16. Canopy _____
17. Acid rain _____
18. Wetlands _____
19. Crepuscular _____
20. Evergreen _____

A Area where an animal or plant finds everything it needs to live.
B Areas of water-clogged soil or area covered with shallow water.
C Partially decomposed organic material.
D Trees that lose leaves.
E Animals or plant of the same species that live in the same area.
F Draining system for water.
G Science of managing forests.
H Particles washed from the land that settle.
I Type of pollution with compounds and water vapor.
J Small pores in leaves and stems.
K Group of interacting plants and animals.
L Active at twilight or sunrise.
M Uppermost layer of forest.
N Process of losing water by plants.
O Freshwater wetland.
P A feature that helps animals or plants survive in a habitat.
Q Take dead material and make it useful as nutrients.
R Show change in environment.
S No longer living.
T Trees that do not lose leaves.

Answers *cover answers if photocopying*

1. F   2. G   3. K   4. S   5. E   6. H   7. N   8. J   9. P   10. A
11. O   12. R   13. C   14. D   15. Q   16. M   17. I   18. B   19. L   20. T

THE ABC's GO...

Name: _____

*Try to remember all the things you learned about Linville Falls.
Working with a friend, write an environmental fact or rule for each letter.*

A. _____
B. _____
C. _____
D. _____
E. _____
F. _____
G. _____
H. _____
I. _____
J. _____
K. _____
L. _____
M. _____
N. _____
O. _____
P. _____
Q. _____
R. _____
S. _____
T. _____
U. _____
V. _____
W. _____
X. _____
Y. _____
Z. _____

KEYING OUT LEAVES

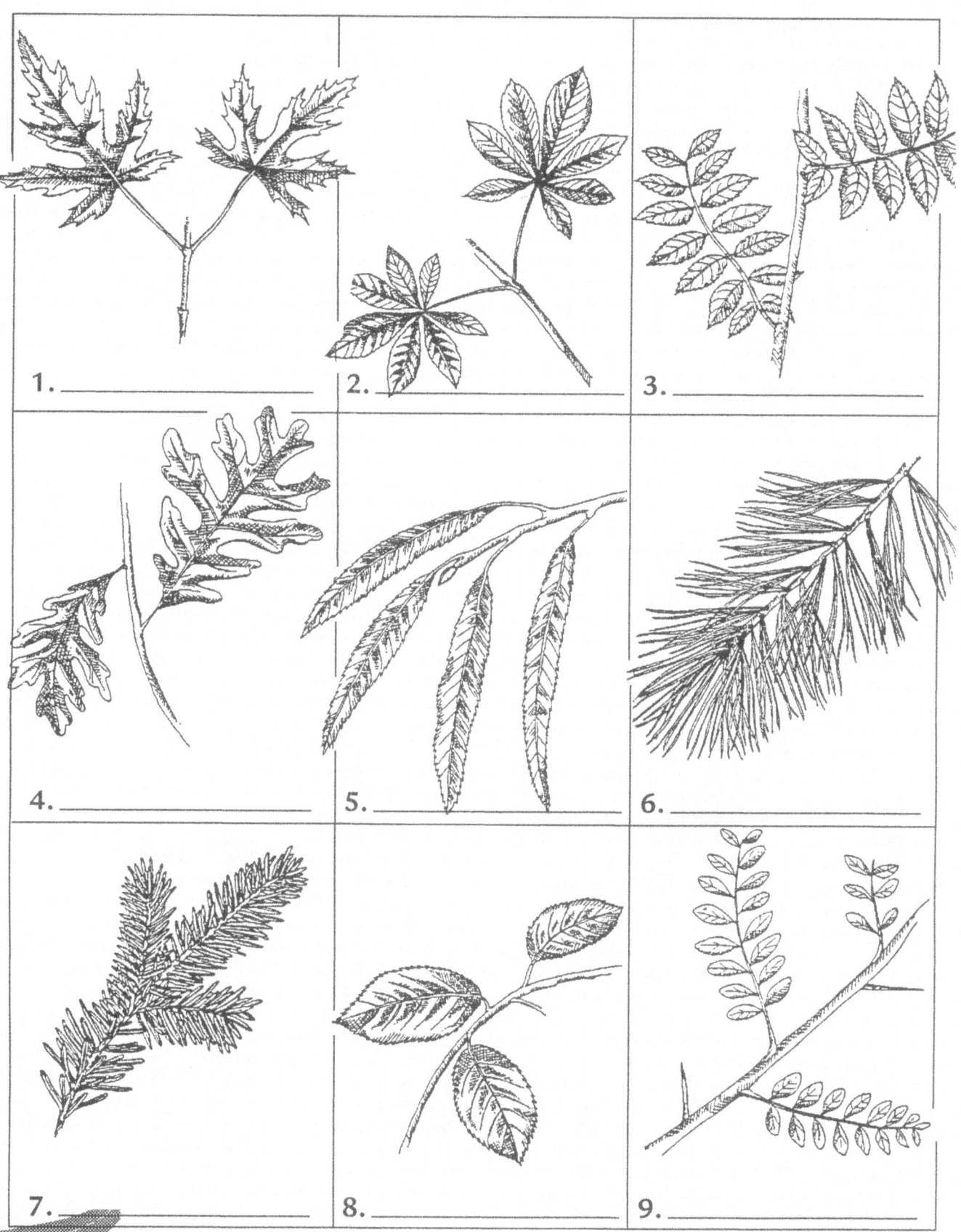

1. _____
2. _____
3. _____
4. _____
5. _____
6. _____
7. _____
8. _____
9. _____

LEAF KEY

1. Leaves are shaped like needles ---------- go to 2
   Leaves are broad and flat ---------- go to 3

2. Long needles grow in bunches of 5 ---------- WHITE SPRUCE
   Needles are short and grow singly along the branch ---------- SITKA SPRUCE

3. Leaves are oposite ---------- go to 4
   Leaves are alternate ---------- go to 5

4. Leaves are simple ---------- SILVER MAPLE
   Leaves are compound ---------- HORSE CHESTNUT

5. Leaves are simple ---------- go to 6
   Leaves are compound ---------- go to 8

6. Leaves are lobes ---------- WHITE OAK
   Leaves are toothed ---------- go to 7

7. Leaves are long and slender ---------- WEEPING WILLOW
   Leaves are rounded ---------- CHOKE CHERRY

8. Branches have thorns ---------- HONEY LOCUST
   Leaflets are toothed ---------- BLACK WALNUT

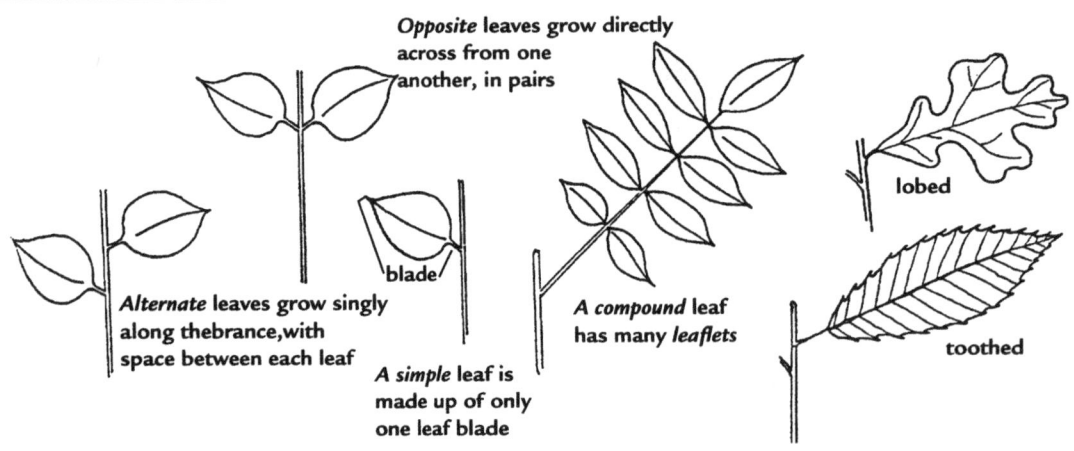

Opposite leaves grow directly across from one another, in pairs

Alternate leaves grow singly along thebrance, with space between each leaf

A simple leaf is made up of only one leaf blade

blade

A compound leaf has many *leaflets*

lobed

toothed

A WALK IN THE WOODS

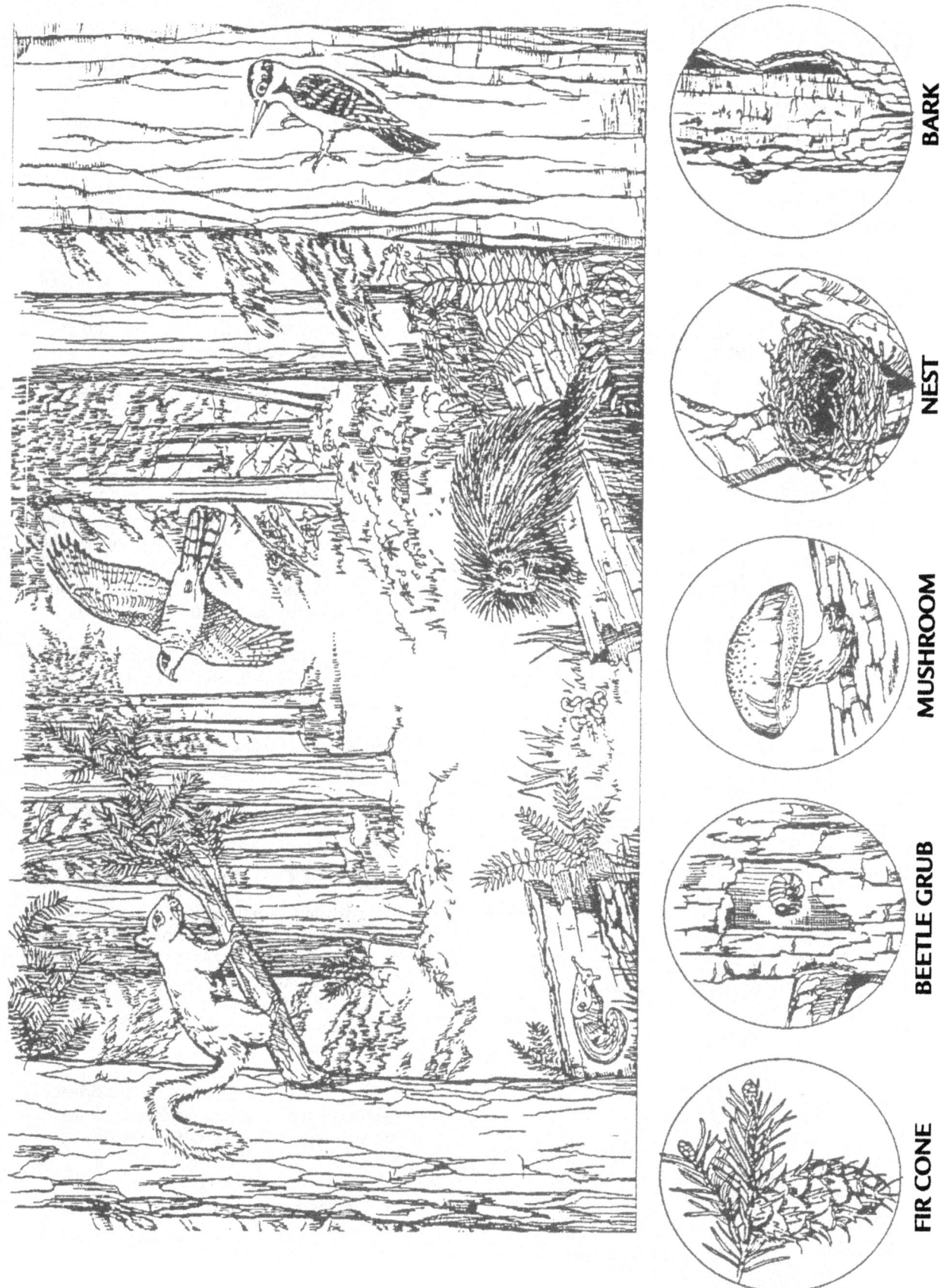

BARK

NEST

MUSHROOM

BEETLE GRUB

FIR CONE

Taken from Ranger Rick Nature scope, "Trees are Terrific"

See what you can find on your walk through the woods. These are only suggestions-- perhaps you will see more.

HOW'S THE WATER UP THERE?

GOALS:
The learner will understand that elevation affects the temperature and precipitation of an area. The learner will compute the basic differences.

OBJECTIVES:
NORTH CAROLINA:
The learner will solve problems and reason immediately.

TENNESSEE:
Use information from tables, charts and graphs to solve problems involving the basic four operations on whole numbers.

PRE-SITE ACTIVITIES:
1. Have students complete the worksheets on elevation and temperature and then discuss the results.

2. Have students design a travel brochure for the Blue Ridge Parkway, featuring one of the sites they find appealing.

3. Have students prepare a class collection of pictures that represent the Blue Ridge Parkway at each season. They could then make seasonal collages.

4. Have each student make a quilt square showing their favorite parkway site.

ON-SITE ACTIVITIES:
1. As the students travel on the parkway, have them record the temperature every 10 miles and create a line graph from this information. The activity should reinforce the condensation rate/temperature relationship.

2. Have students look at outcroppings of rocks on the road banks and tell the type of rock and the rock formation, if possible.

3. Have students use a rock hunter's field manual to identify rocks they see.

4. Stop at the N. C. Mineral Museum.

POST-SITE ACTIVITIES:
1. Have students identify how the mountains were a barrier to the settlement of the western part of the state. Have students use the Knoxville Quadrant topographical map *(at most hiking stores)* to locate gaps the early settlers came through. Discuss the early settlement patterns.

2. Have students research the early pioneers such as Daniel Boone and then look for places on the map named for them.

3. Students may want to do further reading and research.

NORTH CAROLINA RELIEF MAPPING

DIRECTIONS:
A relief map shows elevation of height. On the map, below each letter is an area of the same general elevation. Color all areas with the same letter the same color. For example, color all the A's yellow then go to the key for the map and color the A yellow. Do each letter the same way, choosing different colors for each letter.

ACTIVITY:
Look at the pattern the colors make then answer the following questions.

1. What is the color of the greatest part of the state?

2. Using the map, how many mountains are above 5,500 feet?

3. List the names of these mountains.

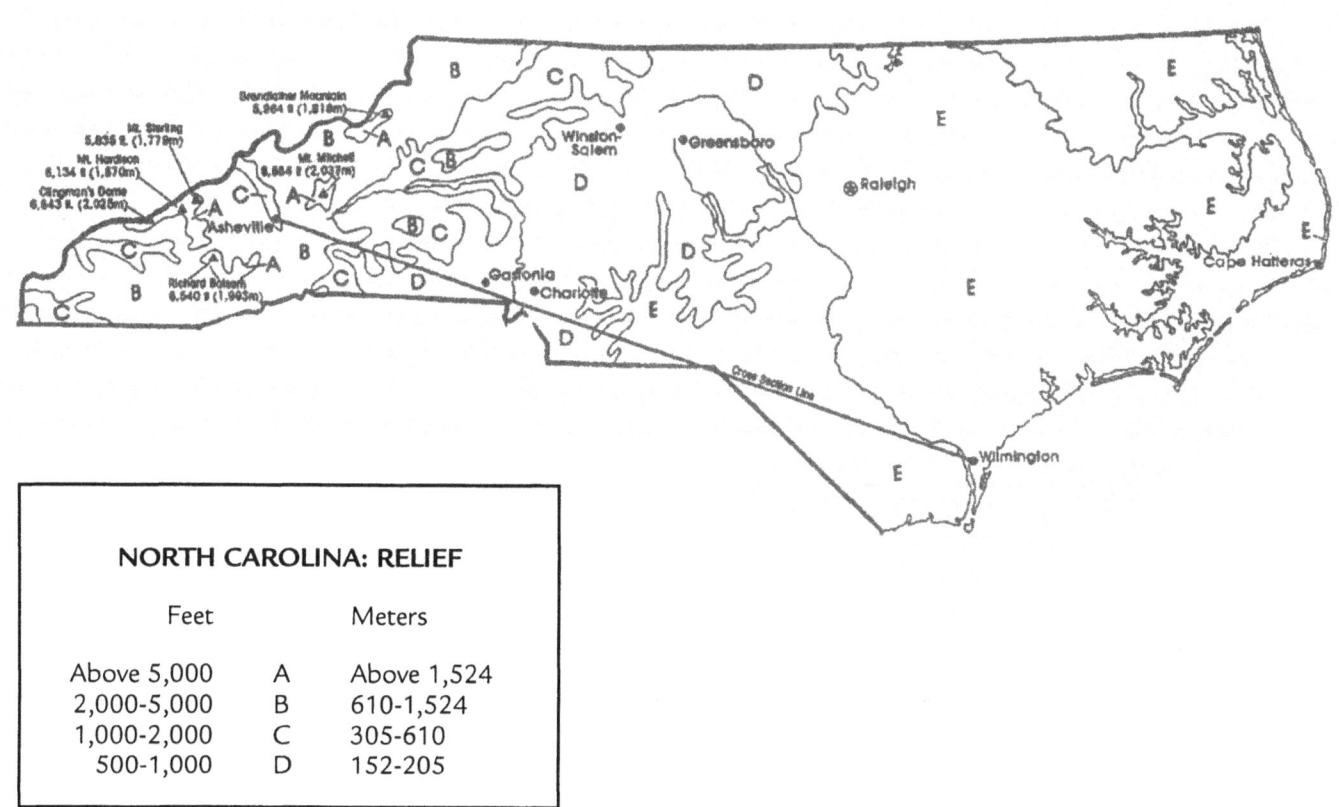

NORTH CAROLINA: RELIEF

Feet		Meters
Above 5,000	A	Above 1,524
2,000-5,000	B	610-1,524
1,000-2,000	C	305-610
500-1,000	D	152-205

NORTH CAROLINA CROSS SECTION

ACTIVITY:

Color each section of the cross section. It is better to use a different color for each section.

A cross section is a way of looking at elevation (height). Look at this cross section from Wilmington to Asheville. Note the rise in elevation as you cross the state. For each rise in elevation of 1,000 feet, there is a 3° drop in temperature. With this in mind, answer the following questions:

1. If the temperature in Wilmington (0 elevation) is 85° what would be the approximate temperature in Asheville? On the Blue Ridge Parkway?

2. How much cooler would it be on Mount Mitchell (6,684 feet). HINT: Multiply then subtract.

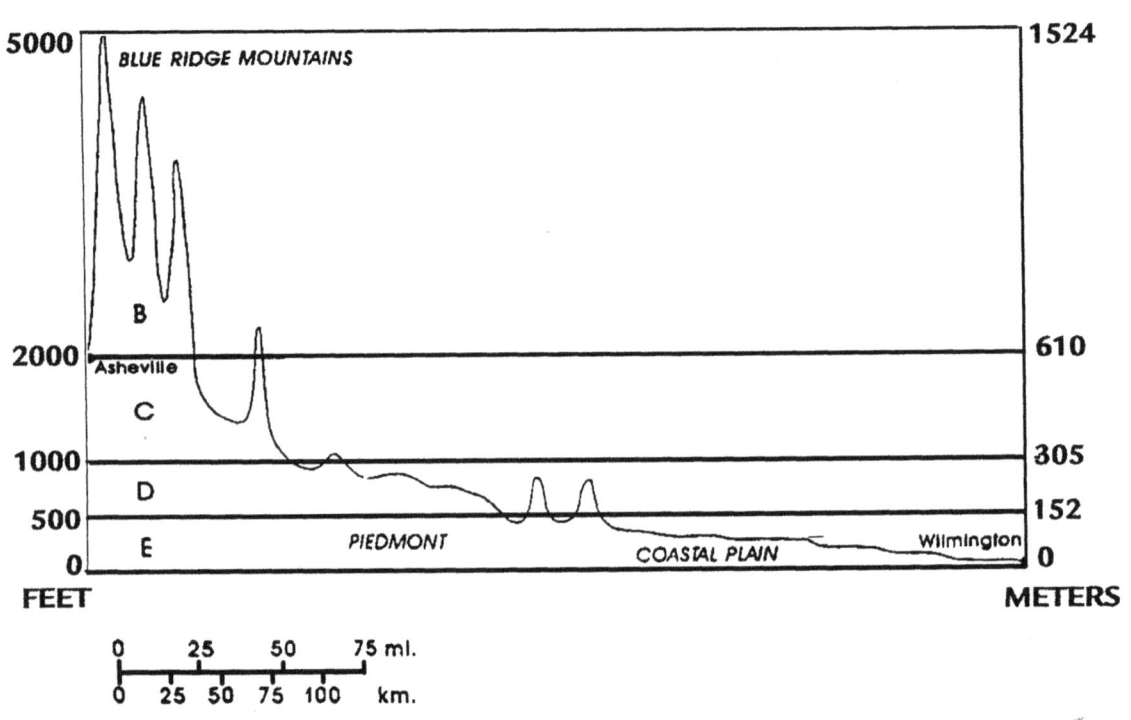

NORTH CAROLINA YEARLY RAINFALL

ACTIVITY:

The map below shows the average yearly rainfall for your state.

Color the boxes in the key, using a different color for each box. Then color all the sections on the map labeled A with the color you used for box A in the key. Color the other sections on the map with the same colors shown in the key.

What is the average yearly rainfall in your part of the state?

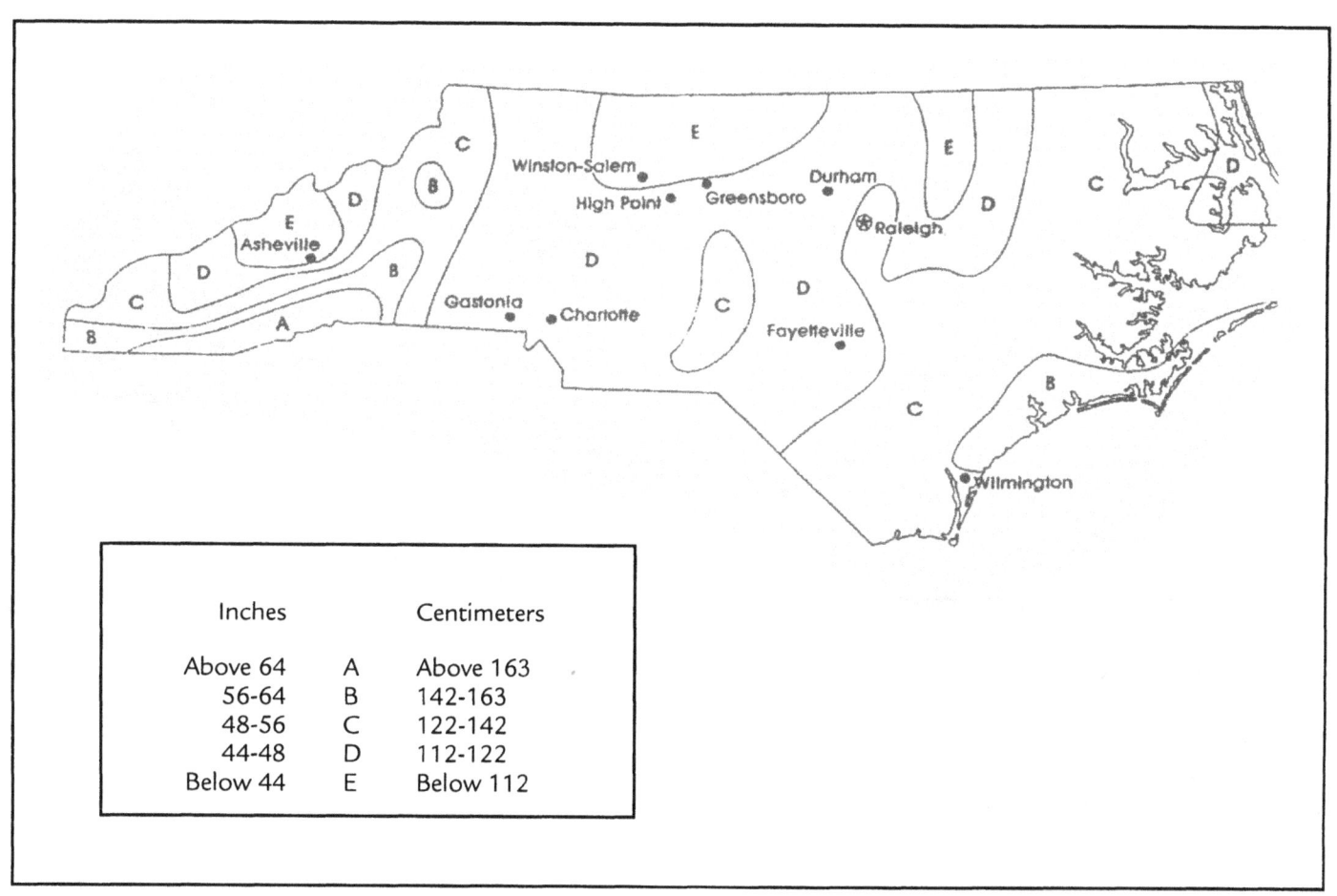

Inches		Centimeters
Above 64	A	Above 163
56-64	B	142-163
48-56	C	122-142
44-48	D	112-122
Below 44	E	Below 112

NORTH CAROLINA YEARLY SNOW FALL

ACTIVITY:

This map shows the average yearly snowfall in your state.

Color the boxes in the key, using a different color for each box. Then color all the sections on the map labeled A with the color you used for box A in the key. Color the other sections on the map with the same colors shown in the key.

What is the average yearly snowfall in your part of the state?

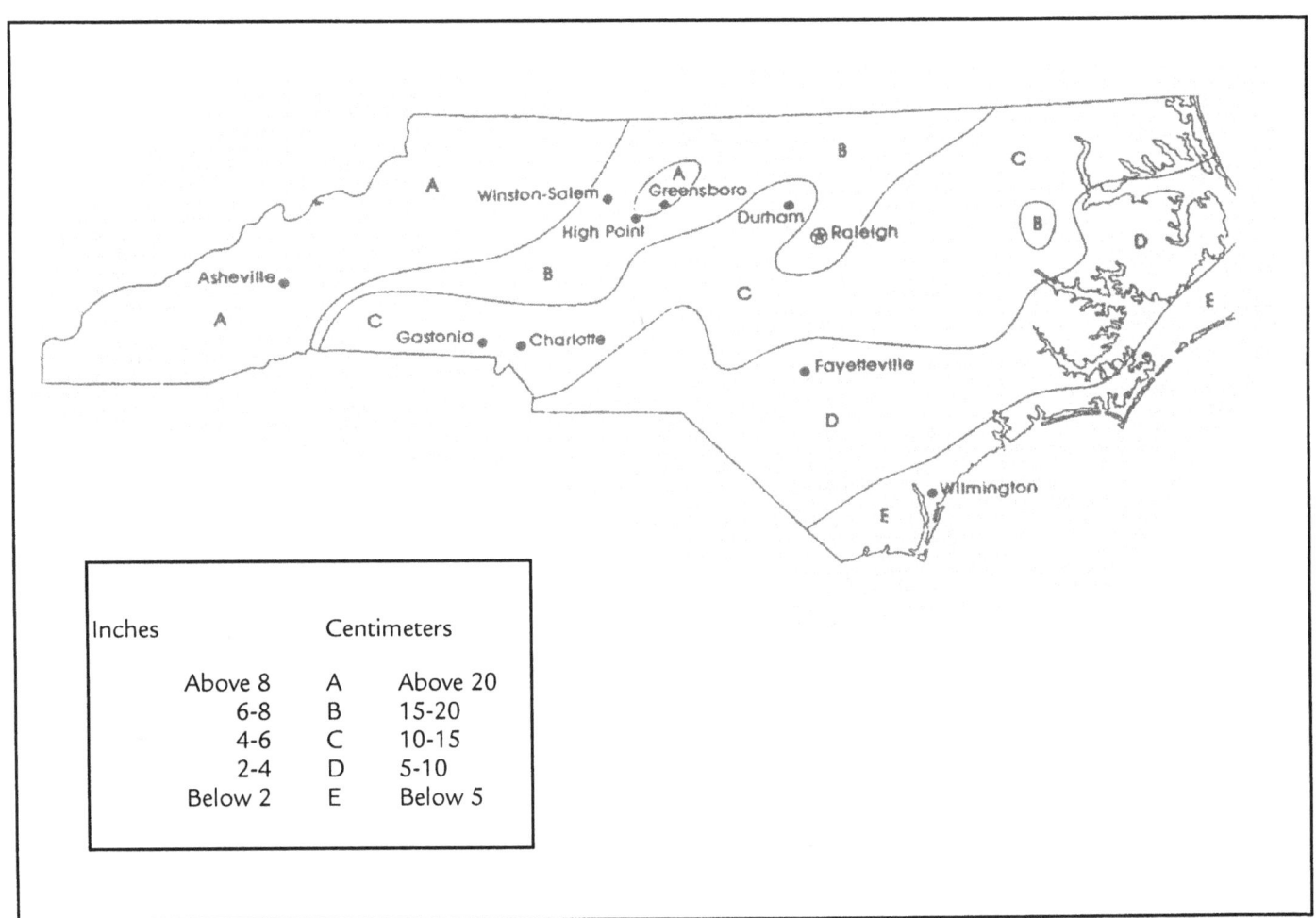

Inches		Centimeters
Above 8	A	Above 20
6-8	B	15-20
4-6	C	10-15
2-4	D	5-10
Below 2	E	Below 5

NORTH CAROLINA AVERAGE JULY TEMPERATURE

ACTIVITY:

This map shows the average July temperature in your state.

Color the boxes in the key, using a different color for each box. Then color all the sections on the map labeled A with the color you used for box A in the key. Color the other sections on the map with the same colors shown in the key.

What is the average July temperature in your part of the state?

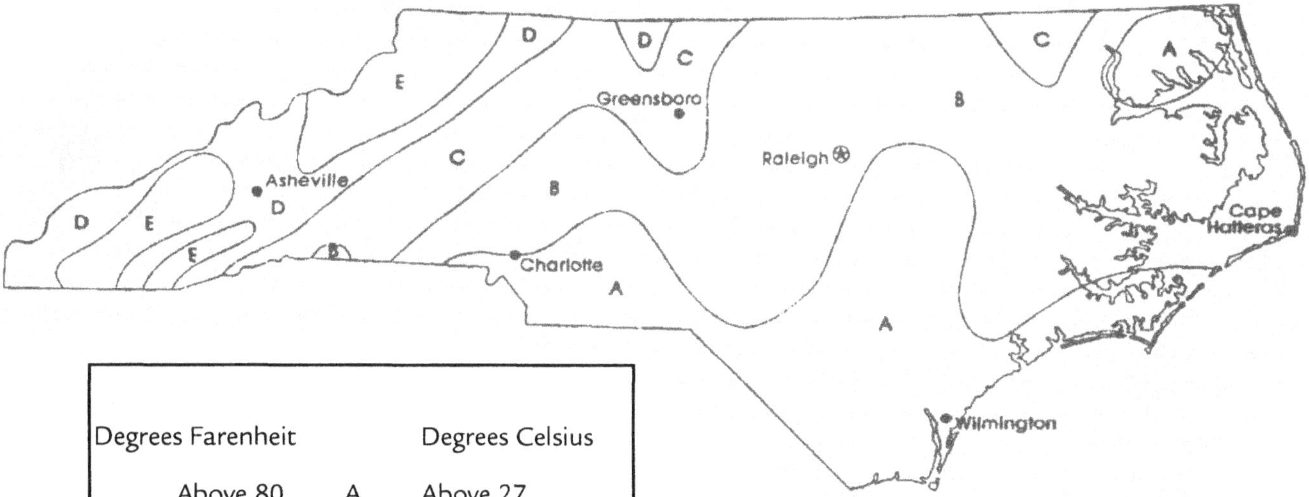

Degrees Farenheit		Degrees Celsius
Above 80	A	Above 27
78-80	B	26-27
76-78	C	24-26
72-76	D	22-24
Below 72	E	Below 22

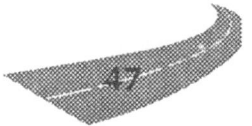

NORTH CAROLINA AVERAGE JANUARY TEMPERATURE

ACTIVITY:

This map shows the average January temperatures in your state.

Color the boxes in the key, using a different color for each box. Then color all the sections on the map labeled A with the color you used for box A in the key. Color the other sections on the map with the same colors shown in the key.

What is the average January temperature in your part of the state?

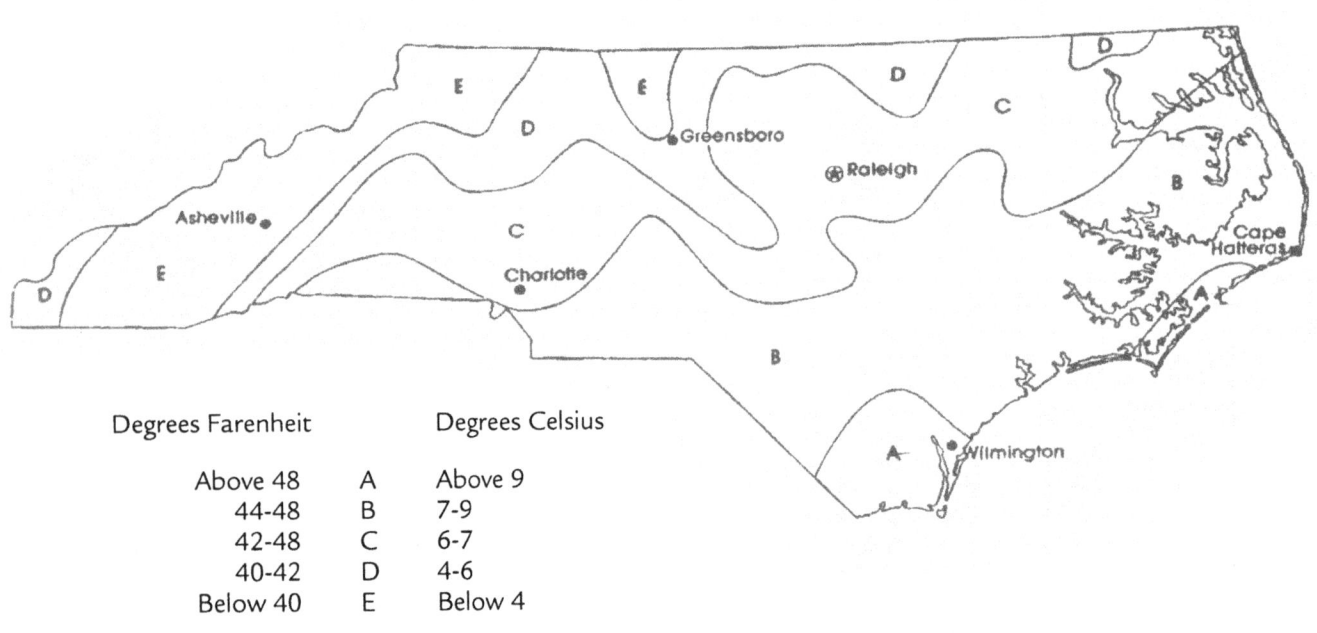

Degrees Farenheit		Degrees Celsius
Above 48	A	Above 9
44-48	B	7-9
42-48	C	6-7
40-42	D	4-6
Below 40	E	Below 4

ROAN MOUNTAIN AND THE APPALACHIAN TRAIL

Pisgah National Forest

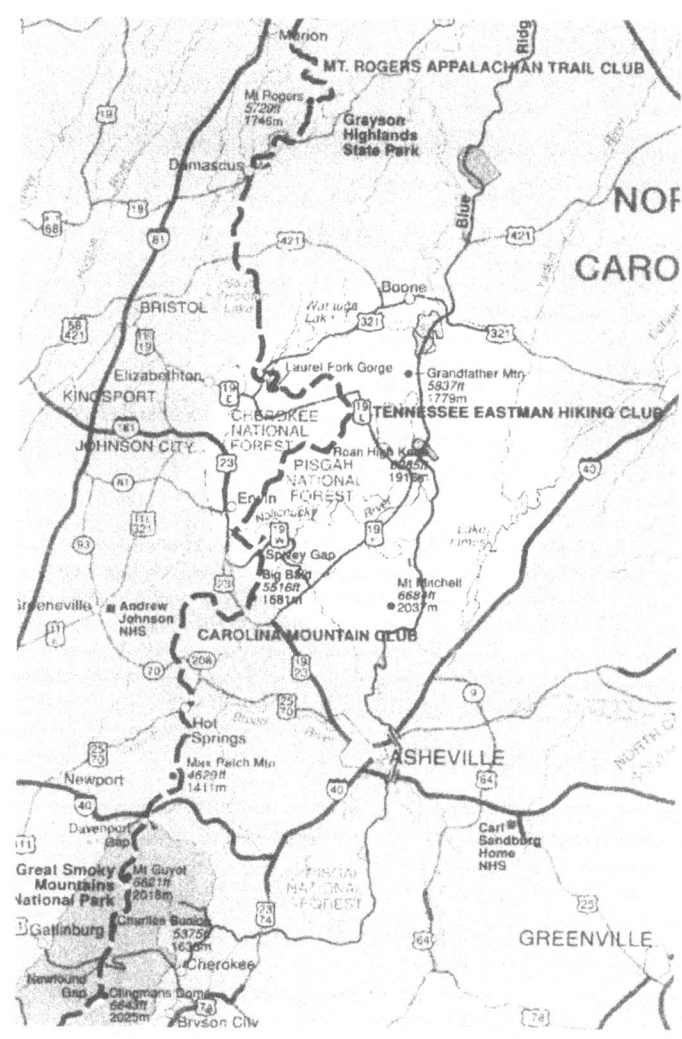

Rising 6,285 feet into the sky, the beauty and majesty of Roan Mountain promises your students a field trip they will never forget. Roan Mountain is not a single peak, but rather a long, high ridge which spreads in waves for more than five miles through Pisgah National Forest over the North Carolina/Tennessee border. The Appalachian Trail follows this wave, taking your students through rhododendron gardens, over rare "balds," and through forests carpeted with wildflowers and ferns. Although the area is isolated and wild, it is within an easy drive of Boone, Banner Elk and Blowing Rock, North Carolina, and Johnson City, Tennessee.

Roan Mountain is famous partly because of its large balds — areas that remain free of trees for no apparent reason. The balds are easily accessible from the Appalachian Trail at Carver's Gap. Another attraction are the Rhododendron Gardens, which bloom in late June. The gardens offer more than 200 acres of catawba rhododendron, the largest such expanse in the United States. The mountain is also rich in history, home to the once famous Cloudland Hotel. Today, it is managed by the National Forest Service and Tennessee State Park System, and is noted as a fine example of wise forest management.

Roan Mountain is a uniquely interesting place. People come to hike the balds, to see the rhododendron in bloom, to enjoy the fall colors, and to camp and picnic. Though it is easily accessible, the Roan is really a world unto itself. We suggest that you try some of the following activities and give your students an experience to treasure.

Directions to Roan Mountain:

From Tennessee: Take Highway 19E from Elizabethton to the village of Roan Mountain. Proceed 22 miles to the top of the mountain by following the prominent signs for Roan Mountain State Park and turning onto Tennessee Highway 143.

From North Carolina (northern counties): Find your way to Elk Park, North Carolina, then follow Highway 19E across the Tennessee line to the village of Roan Mountain. At the signs for the park, follow Tennessee Highway 143 to the summit.

From North Carolina (southern counties): Take North Carolina 261 from Bakersville. North Carolina 261 will meet Tennessee 143 at the state border at the crest of Roan Mountain.

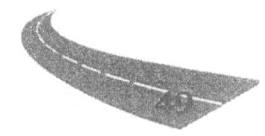

MAPPING THE APPALACHIAN TRAIL

GOAL:
The goal is to give students a sense of the length of the Appalachian Trail and its beauty. The learner will use mapping skills to map the Appalachian Trail.

STATE OBJECTIVES:
STRAND:

Social Studies and Physical Education.

NORTH CAROLINA:

3.11: Locate North Carolina on maps of the United States and of the world using latitude and longitude designations.

TENNESSEE:

Recognize that natural regions are represented on different types of maps by using physical features, climate, vegetation and natural resources. Use longitudinal and latitudinal lines to locate natural regions on the maps.

BACKGROUND INFORMATION:
Students will need to research the Appalachian Mountains and trails. Have students to find out the beginning and ending points of the mountain trail. They will need to collect longitude and latitude points of these locations. They also will need to find the length of the trail.

The Appalachian Trail is 2,168 miles stretching from Springer Mountain in Georgia to Mount Katahdin in Northern Maine. The trail is the longest continuously marked hiking trail in the world, stretching through 14 states. It is not an easy walk and was created for serious hikers who want a physical challenge while enjoying spectacular scenery.

ACTIVITIES:
Find two maps with the eastern half of the United States or use the maps included. One map needs latitude and longitude lines on it, and the other should show mountain ranges.

Have students find Roan Mountain on the latitude and longitude map at 82° west latitude and 36° north longitude. Have students mark Roan Mountain with a marker. Have students mark the trail first with a pencil and, after being checked, use a marker to highlight the trail. The teacher can check one student in each row and then let the students check everyone else in their row.

Have the students take the maps with them on the field trip. Students should mark the area hiked with a different color marker. Record the time it takes to hike the trail. Upon returning to the classroom, have students calculate how long it would take them to hike the entire trail.

Other points to plot:

1. Springer Mountain, Georgia
   84 W latitude and 34 N longitude

2. Erwin, Tennessee
   83 W latitude and 35 1/2 N longitude

3. Roan Mountain, Tennessee
   82 W latitude and 36 N longitude

4. Turner's Gap, Maryland
   78 W latitude and 39 3/4 N longitude

5. Southern New York
   74 3/4 W latitude and 42 N longitude

6. White Mountains, New Hampshire
   44 N latitude and 73 W longitude

7. Mt. Katahdin, Maine
   46 N latitude and 69 W longitude

Resource: Silver, Burdett and Ginn, Science Textbook.

MAPPING THE APPALACHIAN TRAIL

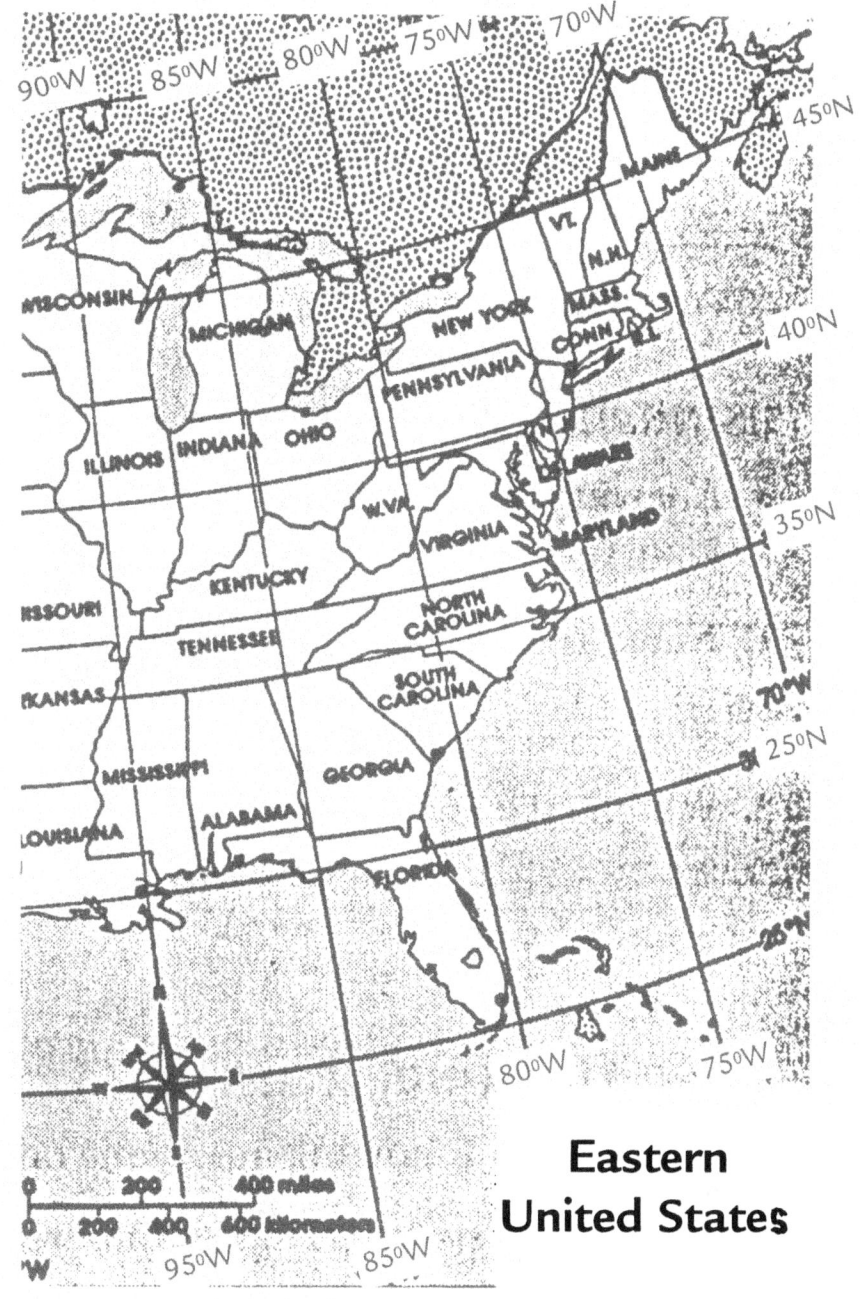

Eastern United States

MAPPING THE APPALACHIAN TRAIL ANSWERS

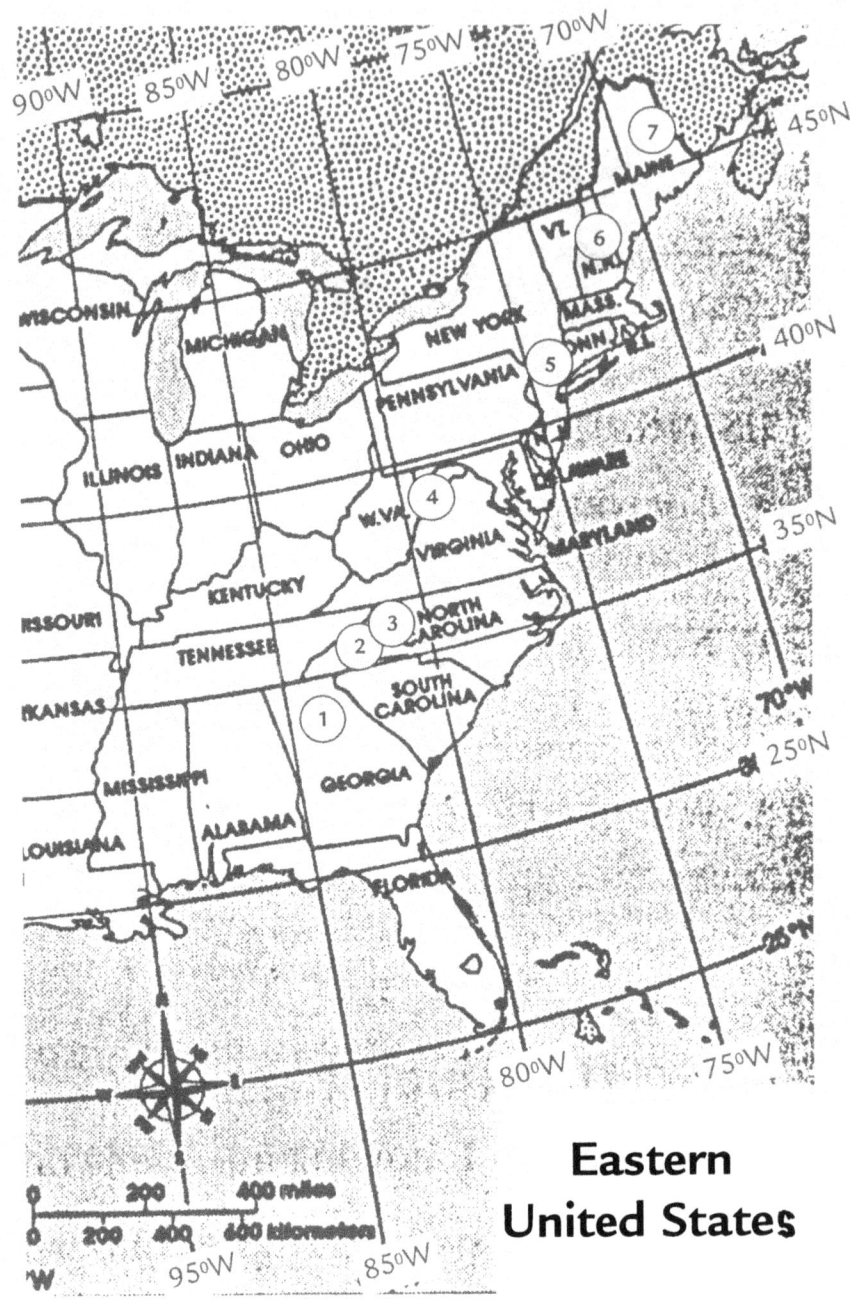

Eastern United States

EXTRA, EXTRA! READ ALL ABOUT IT!

GOAL:
The learner will be aware of the relationship between the history of a region and its location, natural setting, natural resources and natural changes.

STATE OBJECTIVES:
NORTH CAROLINA:

LANGUAGE ARTS AND SOCIAL STUDIES:

2.2: The learner will analyze, synthesize and organize information and discover related ideas, concepts or generalizations.

2.3: The learner will apply, extend and expand on information and concepts.

5: The learner will evaluate ways the people of North Carolina use, modify and adapt to the physical environment.

The learner will write a newspaper article about the rare Gray's Lily found on Roan Mountain.

The learner will use correct capitalization and punctuation.

ACTIVITY:
Pass out copies of "Rare Gray's Lily at Home on Roan", included. Read and discuss articles together. Complete summary sheet.

Inform students that they are to be a reporter and write a story in the Earth Smart Newspaper about the discovery of Gray's Lily. The article should contain a headline, illustration and byline. The article should contain information about:

Who is Asa Gray?

Description of the lily

Location of its growth

Reasons for the plant's rarity

Solutions for its continuation

MATERIALS:
Newspaper article "Rare Gray's Lily at Home on Roan" in Johnson City Press (July 3, 1995)

Earth Smart News activity sheet

"Rare Gray's Lily at Home on Roan" activity sheet, summary sheet

EXTRA, EXTRA! READ ALL ABOUT IT!

RARE GRAY'S LILY AT HOME ON ROAN

BY MICHAEL JOSLIN

ROAN MOUNTAIN — As early summer establishes itself on the verdant balds, among the wind-rippled green and gold grasses can be seen glowing bits of flame - the blossoms of the Gray's Lily or Roan Lily.

This fiery flower with its combination of beauty and rarity has become an important part of the heritage of the Roan Highlands.

Gray's Lily links today to the distant past. It is a rare plant that exists naturally in only a few areas. The Roan is its main habitat. The lily was discovered there, and the main population of this nationally significant plant exists there today. As the balds go, so goes the lily.

Keeping the balds clear of woody vegetation is a major problem today. The ways in which this distinctive flower reacts mark the relative success of the means used to preserve the unique character of the grassy balds.

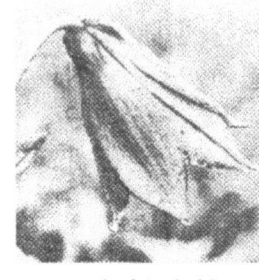

Jewel of the balds

In prehistoric times, large herbivores kept the balds clear of woody species that eventually would have turned these high-elevation meadows into forest. According to Wake Forest University, Winston-Salem, N. C., mammoths and mastodons, as well as ground sloths, horses, peccaries, caribou, moose, muskoxen and bison, "ranged the Southern Appalachians."

"The impact of these species individually and collectively on the regional vegetation was very likely quite spectacular," wrote Weigl in his proposal Southern Appalachian Grassy Balds: Rethinking Both Origins and Management.

Over the millennia, grazing animals kept the balds open. The Indians hunted the herds, and later the white settlers would drive their own livestock to fatten in the summer on the luxuriant grasses.

In late June and early July of 1841, the pioneering American botanist Asa Gray traveled through parts of the Southern Appalachians to study and collect plant specimens. While dazzled by the incredible wealth and diversity of plants in the region, he was equally impressed by the scenic beauty of the open meadows and the mountains on all sides.

He ascended the Roan after climbing Grandfather Mountain. "It was just sunset when we reached the bald and grassy summit of this noble mountain, and after enjoying for a moment the magnificent view it affords, had barely time to prepare out encampment," Gray wrote in an article published shortly after his trip to our mountains.

One of the plants he identified on this trip was the lilium canadense. According to Jim Massey, director of the

Discovered last century growing in the Roan Mountain balds, the Gray's Lily is a rare flower that relies on the bald's lack of woody vegetation. Growth of blackberries and alders hampers the plant's chance for success, and the United States Forest Service is exploring ways to keep the balds clear so the lilies can flourish. Left, a Gray's Lily blossom is covered with morning dew; below, botanist Asa Gray, for whom the lily is named, probably first noticed it on an 1841 expedition to the area.

herbarium at the University of North Carolina at Chapel Hill, this species of lily closely resembles the Gray's Lily. Gray may have discovered the plant that bears his name on this first visit, but he failed to distinguish it from its near relative.

In 1879, his protege Sereno Watson officially described the flower and named it for his mentor.

During the 19th century and much of this century, livestock kept the balds open on the Roan Highlands and thus kept the Gray's Lily in a flourishing state. Cleo Edwards grew up on a farm below the balds and spent much of his recreation time among the herds on the meadows. He knew the lilies and saw them in the 1930's, 40's and 50's.

"Yes, they was plenty of them," Cleo said. "It seems like they done a lot better than they do now. The stock kept everything picked down around them."

After the U. S. Forest Service acquired the balds during the middle decades of this century, the government stopped the grazing. Shortly thereafter, the slow but steady process of woodland encroachment began. As the blackberry briars and alders flourished, the Gray's Lilies declined.

In the past two decades, the Forest Service has tried many different ways to prevent the disappearance of the unique habitat of the balds. Fire, chemicals, weed mowers and other means have been employed with little permanent success.

Then, for three years a herd of goats was given part of the job.

"We have found that where we grazed with the goats, the following year we found hundreds of Gray's Lily seedlings where they had not been before," said Frank Roth, a ranger for the Toecane District of the Pisgah National Forest that oversees the balds.

"When we kept the goats out of that place the next year, the blackberries came back and shaded the lilies out," Roth said. "Where we let the goat's graze, there were still hundreds of them. We're putting in plots and doing more monitoring of what's happening there now."

The goats are gone this year; last summer was the third of a three-year test program. Time will tell how quickly the briars and other woody species overshadow the lilies.

EXTRA, EXTRA! READ ALL ABOUT IT!

SUMMARY SHEET

1. What is the "Jewel of the Bald"?

2. Who discovered it?

3. When was it discovered?

4. What is another name for Gray's Lily?

5. The Gray's Lily relies on the balds' lack of _____.

6. In prehistoric times, large _____ kept the balds clear of woody species.

7. In pioneer days, the _____ kept balds clear.

8. Today, as the _____ flourished, the Gray's Lilies declined.

9. What organization has tried to help save the Gray's Lily?

10. What has this organization tried to do to stop the growth of other plants that are killing the lilies? Name three.

11. What animals were used to get rid of unwanted plants on the balds?

ANSWERS
1. The Gray's Lily
2. Asa Gray
3. 1841
4. Roan Lily
5. Woody vegetation
6. Herbivores
7. Livestock or grazing animals
8. Blackberry briars and/or alders
9. United States Forest Service
10. Fire, Chemicals, Weed mowers
11. Goats

EXTRA, EXTRA! READ ALL ABOUT IT!

EARTH SMART NEWS

*SPECIAL EDITION
FOR ENVIRONMENTAL ISSUES*

HEADLINE:

BYLINE

ROAN: A MOUNTAIN OF OPPORTUNITY

GOAL:
The learner will understand the relationship between the history of a region and its location, natural setting, natural resources and natural changes and its effect on the economy of the region.

STATE OBJECTIVES:
NORTH CAROLINA:

GOAL 5: The learner will evaluate ways the people of North Carolina use, modify and adapt to the physical environment.

5.2: Describe how North Carolinians now use, modify or adapt to their physical environment.

5.3: Analyze causes and consequences of the misuse of the physical environment and propose alternatives.

GOAL 11: The learner will assess changes in ways of living over time and investigate why and how these changes occurred.

11.3: Evaluate the effects of change on the lives of the people of North Carolina.

ACTIVITY:
The Roan High Knob area is a unique land of resources and opportunities. Although people are aware of its scenic and recreational aspects, the Roan also has an economic tradition.

Below are some of the resources that have been of economic value to the people living in the area. Describe how each contributed to the local economy. If possible, try to locate and identify the plants.

APPALACHIAN TRAIL
FRASER FIR
GALAX
"PINE" CONES
THE FOREST
CATAWBA RHODODENDRON
GRASSY AND HEATH BALDS
GINSENG
CRANBERRY CREEK IRON
MICA
CHAMPION COMPANY
ROAN MOUNTAIN STATE PARK

MATERIALS:
Note pad
Plant identification book
Roan Mountain State Park brochure
Copy of Roan High Knob Area Analysis
Book: Wilson, Jennifer. *Roan Mountain: A Passage of Time*

DISCUSSION:
The National Forest Service manages the Roan High Knob area. How are they trying to maintain the distinctive qualities of Roan Mountain, such as plants, wildlife and human needs? What suggestions do you have for preserving and enjoying the beauty of the area?

Choose from the list above what you think had the most destructive influence on Roan Mountain. Give your reasons. Explain what you consider the most important use of the Roan High Knob area today.

ROAN: A MOUNTAIN OF OPPORTUNITY

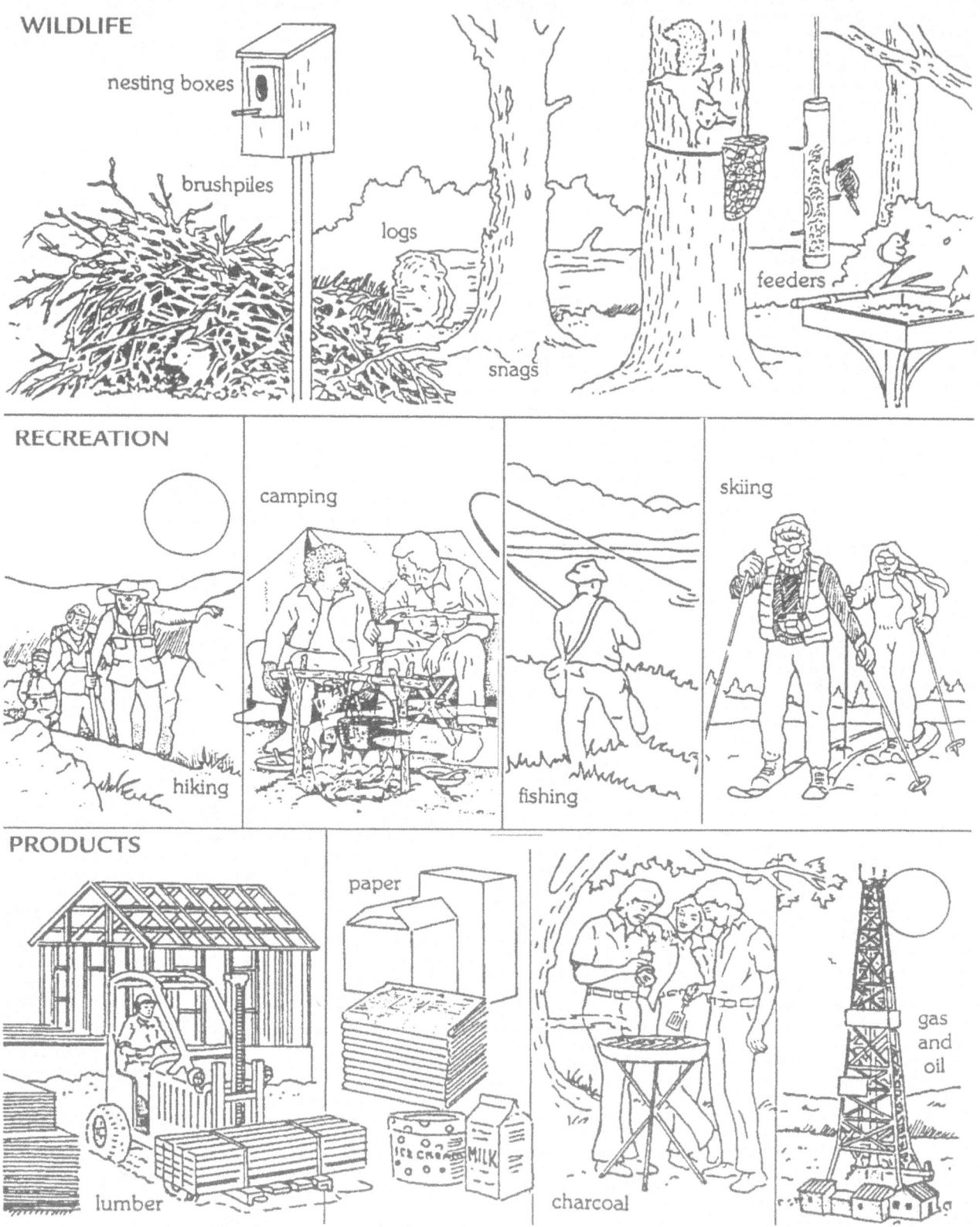

These pictures represent aspects of forest management. Debate which ones might be appropriate on Roan Mountain.

Taken from Ranger Rick Nature scope, "Trees are Terrific"

ROAN: A MOUNTAIN OF OPPORTUNITY

   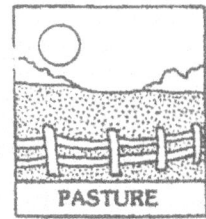 

DAMS — FURNITURE — ROADS — PASTURE — FOOD

1. FILLING & DRAINING WETLANDS   2. CUTTING DOWN FORESTS   3. OVERGRAZING LIVESTOCK

LUMBER — BUILDINGS — WOOL/LEATHER — FARMS — FIREWOOD

Forest products and use–Discuss aspects of each.

ROAN WORD SEARCH

```
D X B X G W T P B R B O T A N Y K V Z K
V E R Q J S B L Y F C C L O U D L A N D
I F F B S W X P F A G Z Z U X H U R G A
R X Q O Y J F S N O P V F Y H W O L A B
S E W Y R F L O Y G R P S S D S B I R W
I W Z W O E P T T X B E M O E B I A D A
L E N X Y Y S W N R J H S T H Q X R E T
V Q U J I F O T W E E S R T R Y M T N A
I Q W G N O X C A K E E L A R H V N S C
C Y Q A D R J H H T E R Z X T Y E A G R
U C C C T Q Z K Z D I R G S V A I I F N
L N I A T N U O M N A O R R K C Z H H P
T R H O D O D E N D R O N L E U M C N D
U L B O I S U C C E S S I O N V B A R Y
R H S U O U D I C E D M Q N U S E L B J
E X O N O V E R L O O K U K J T M A H U
B F D F M L D L J B A L D B Y H U P W A
Y R R E B K C A L B X O U Z W D G P B J
X G S Y L I L S Y A R G F P K N R A E R
D N T N E M E G A N A M E S U I T L U M
```

WORD LIST

APPALACHIANTRAIL	BALD	BLACKBERRY
BOTANY	CANOPY	CATAWBA
CLOUDLAND	DECIDUOUS	DEFORESTATION
EVERGREEN	FORESTRY	GARDENS
GRAYSLILY	MULTIUSEMANAGEMENT	OVERLOOK
RHODODENDRON	ROANMOUNTAIN	ROSETREE
SILVICULTURE	SUCCESSION	

_____ _____ _____ _____ _____

_____ _____ _____ _____ _____

_____ _____ _____ _____ _____

ROAN WORD SEARCH ANSWERS

```
         D . . . . . . . . . B O T A N Y . . . .
         . E . . . . . . . . C C L O U D L A N D
         . . F . . . . F A . . . . . . R G A
         . . . O . . . N O . . . . . O L A B
         S . . R . O . . R . . . S . I R W
         I . . . E P . . . E . E . . A D A
         L . . . Y S . N . . S T . . . R E T
         V . . . . . T . E . . R T . . . T N A
         I . . . . . . A . E E . . R . . N S C
         C . . . . . . . T E R . . . Y . A . .
         U . . . . . . . . I . G . . . I . .
         L N I A T N U O M N A O R R . . . H . .
         T R H O D O D E N D R O N . E . . C . .
         U . . . S U C C E S S I O N V . A . .
         R . S U O U D I C E D . . . . . E L . .
         E . . . O V E R L O O K . . . . . A . .
         . . . . . . . . B A L D . . . . P . .
         Y R R E B K C A L B . . . . . . . P . .
         . . . Y L I L S Y A R G . . . . . A . .
         . . T N E M E G A N A M E S U I T L U M
```

WORD LIST

APPALACHIANTRAIL	BALD	BLACKBERRY
BOTANY	CANOPY	CATAWBA
CLOUDLAND	DECIDUOUS	DEFORESTATION
EVERGREEN	FORESTRY	GARDENS
GRAYSLILY	MULTIUSEMANAGEMENT	OVERLOOK
RHODODENDRON	ROANMOUNTAIN	ROSETREE
SILVICULTURE	SUCCESSION	

SCAVENGER HUNT or BINGO

GOAL:
The learner will construct an understanding of science concepts by analyzing systems. The learner will recognize the differences among animals.

STATE OBJECTIVES:

NORTH CAROLINA:

SCIENCE 5.1: Explore the groupings of animals

SCIENCE 5.1.1: Using characteristics, classify into groups animals such as invertebrates, reptiles, mammals, amphibians, fish and insects

TENNESSEE:

SCIENCE: The learner will recognize the differences among animals.

ACTIVITY:
This identification sheet can be used in a variety of ways. Students may use it as a scavenger hunt and try to find as many of these living things as possible or it can be used as a form of bingo, in which students attempt to find items to make a vertical, horizontal or diagonal line. Students may be asked to locate all mammals shown on the sheet, etc.

SCAVENGER HUNT

DOGWOOD   **CARDINAL**   **GRAY SQUIRREL**   **GALAX**

TURKEY VULTURE   **DEER**   **POISON IVY**   **OAK TREE**

WHITE PINE   **BEAVER**   **OPOSSUM**   **TRILLIUM**

WOODCHUCK   **RACCOON**   **FELLED BEAVER TREE**

SURVIVAL AT ITS BEST

GOAL:
The learner will evaluate survival information and learn basic trail and hiking safety.

OBJECTIVE:
To encourage the responsible use of our natural parks and wildlife areas and to develop a caring attitude toward our natural resources.

STATE OBJECTIVES:
NORTH CAROLINA:

SCIENCE:

2.7.5: Discuss how humans must care for the environment to ensure that animals remain healthy and species survive.

SOCIAL STUDIES:

5: The learner will evaluate ways the people of North Carolina use, modify and adapt to the physical environment.

TENNESSEE:

SCIENCE :

Realize how individuals affect the environment.

SOCIAL STUDIES:

Be aware of ways people affect natural resources.

PRE-SITE ACTIVITY:
Bring to class and have students bring articles about people who have been rescued after having been hiking. Conduct with the class a discussion of safety and what you would need to do if you became lost. Divide the class into teams and have them design a safety pack to take with them on a hiking trip so that if you became lost you would know what to do. Have the teams report to the class and then vote on the best plans and survival kits.

ON-SITE ACTIVITY:
Have the students keep a journal of all the possible accidents and ways that their plans would have worked. Again as you begin to hike stress safety and then let the students enjoy the beauty of their surroundings. Let them decide the part they liked best and as they take a break jot some notes for later use. Once again a camera or a video camera would be a useful thing to have.

POST SITE ACTIVITY
Take the things the students observed and design some scenarios and give to the teams and have them play out the best survival scenario. Have them evaluate the difference between the real hike and the make believe one.

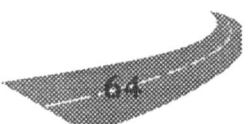

ENVIRONMENTAL MANAGEMENT

GOAL:
To study a managed forest and realize that careful planning and management is practiced to ensure sensitive species survive.

STATE OBJECTIVE:
NORTH CAROLINA:

2.7.5: Discuss how humans must care for the environment to ensure that animals remain healthy and species survive.

TENNESSEE:

To realize how individuals effect the environment.

BACKGROUND INFORMATION:

The Appalachian Mountains were formed approximately 400 million years ago, when the moving continental plates of North America and Africa collided along what is now the east coast of the United States. The entire process of buckling and fracturing and uplifting is thought to have taken about 50 million years.

The rocks that make up Roan Mountain actually predate the formation of the Appalachians. The oldest variety is called Cranberry Gneiss. Dated at more than a billion years, it is among the oldest rocks to be found in the United States. Geologists believe that the peaks in the vicinity of Roan Mountain may have been as high as 20,000 to 30,000 feet before the slow process of glaciation and erosion brought them to their present height. It is glaciation that is given a large share of the credit for the Roan's unique flora. The glaciers extended their principle effect in the Spruce-Fir forest that is found along the 5,000-foot level giving rise to an area of unusual vegetation known as the "Canadian zone." A notable example of the "Canadian zone" is the Rhododendron garden located past Roan High Knob toward the southwest part of the Roan.

There are two basic types of balds with numerous variations. Areas populated by grasses, weeds and wild flowers are known as grass balds. Areas that support the growth of shrubs are called heath balds. The Rhododendron gardens constitute the major shrub bald on Roan Mountain. The grass balds are more extensive, and they are all situated northwest of Carver's Gap. Roan Bald, Jane Bald and Hump Mountain are located on long broad ridges above the 5,500 feet elevation mark. They cover an area of more than a 1,000 acres, mostly with southern exposure. Balds are not static; plant succession does occur on them.

Roan High Knob is a unique and sensitive ecosystem that attracts visitors from around the world. The natural forest lands in the Roan High Knob area are administered by the Cherokee (Tennessee) and the Pisgah (North Carolina) National Forests and are a part of the U.S. Forest Service's planned management area. The forest plan provides management guidance for the maintenance and preservation of the unique ecosystems of the area.

A part of the Appalachian Trail goes through the area also. The area is to be managed to maintain distinctive outstanding scenic quality, wildlife and plant communities as well as the Spruce-Fir and hardwood forest. The goals are to manage the area to appear natural, while maintaining the natural ecosystems and protecting the habitat for threatened and endangered species.

ENVIRONMENTAL MANAGEMENT

PRE-SITE ACTIVITIES:

1. Research the effect of the logging industry on the area and on the environment.

2. How did the early settlers use the grass balds? Did this effect the environment?

3. Look at the natural secession process and decide whether this is what the general public really wants.

4. Study the Forest Service's Management Plan for the Roan areas and then discuss:
    - Appalachian Trail uses and maintenance
    - The harvest of Fraser Fir seedlings
    - Cone picking
    - Cross-country skiing
    - Hiking trails
    - Recreational use

5. Debate the following issues:
    - Protection of rare species and their habitats.
    - Recreational use of National Forest Lands.
    - Protection and maintenance of the Rhododendron Gardens and the balds.

ON-SITE ACTIVITIES:

1. Have the students observe as many examples as possible of planned management and then list specific ways they are helpful.

2. As the students walk on the trails, have them identify the following:
    - Wild strawberries
    - Spreading avens
    - Goosberry
    - Mountain oatgrass
    - Sedge
    - Yarrow
    - Bluets (Quaker ladies)
    - Hair cap moss
    - Lichen
    - Catawba Rhododendron
    - Saxifrages
    - Red Spruce
    - Fraser Fir
    - Mountain Ash
    - Sand Myrtle

POST-SITE ACTIVITIES:

1. Divide the students into groups and have each group devise a management plan for the Roan Mountain area. Possible group assignments:
    - The Appalachian Trail
    - The Rhododendron garden
    - The Balds
    - Recreational use of the area

2. Have students write letters to the National Forest Service thanking them for their work and the opportunity to visit the site.

3. Have students write their representative urging continued support for the National Forest Service.

4. Have students make a mural depicting the parts of a forest management plan.

ENVIRONMENTAL MANAGEMENT

INTRODUCTION:

In the 1800's, the forest was exploited as an inexhaustible resource. Today the forest industry plans for the future. Modern forest planning includes reforestation projects, research on tree diseases and land-use protection. To ensure a continuous crop of trees for future use, logging practices, such as select-cutting and clear-cutting, are used to reduce competition between replantings and the mature trees. Cones are harvested to ensure seedlings for future forests.

PRE-SITE ACTIVITIES:

1. Make a list of all the ways we use trees.

2. If trees were harvested what could be done to prevent erosion?

3. The Christmas tree industry is a growing economic factor in the area. How does it effect the economy, and what is its future?

4. Complete the worksheets on "Measure a Tree" and "Observe a Tree."

MEASURE A TREE ACTIVITY:

1. Measure your tree.
   How many hands around?
   How many footsteps around?

   Now measure with the tape measure.
   How many inches around?

2. Measure the shadow of your tree.
   How many feet long?
   What is the time of day?
   Will this affect your measure? Explain why.

3. Native Americans measured the height of trees in the following manner.

   Walk away from the tree until you can see the top of the tree, while holding you ankles and viewing through your legs. Then turn and pace off the distance from where you are standing to the base of the tree. This is equal to the height of the tree. (Note this is based on the assumption that the angle formed by this sighting is 45 degrees).

   Now you try. Record your answer.

MATERIALS:

Tape measure
Paper

ENVIRONMENTAL MANAGEMENT

OBSERVE A TREE ACTIVITY:

1. View the tree from a distance. Sketch the tree on this page.

2. Observe the tree up close. Touch the tree. Describe the:

   Bark

   Leaves

   Branches

3. What are the colors of your tree?

4. What unusual features does your tree have?

5. Write a paragraph to help others see your tree. Using as many descriptive picture words, adjectives as you can.

CONES AND NEEDLES ACTIVITY:

Observe a cone, branch and some needles from different conifers (pine, spruce, hemlock and fir). Then answer the following questions and make a drawing of each category:

1. Observe cones from the different trees and describe each cone.

   Look

   Feel

   Smell

2. Examine each needle and describe each cone.

   Look

   Arrangement

3. Measure the cones and count the number of scales.

   Length

   Circumference

   Count

   Seed

4. Is there any evidence of disease?

MATERIALS:
Ruler
Tape measure
Pencil
Paper

APPALACHIAN TRAIL PATCH DESIGN

GOALS:
Students will design an Appalachian Trail patch depicting a plant, animal or environmental issue.

STATE OBJECTIVES:
NORTH CAROLINA:
SCIENCE:
2.7.5: Students will discuss how humans must care for the environment to ensure that animals remain healthy and that species survive.

INTRODUCTION:
The Appalachian Trail is the longest continuously marked hiking trail in the world. It stretches unbroken for 2,168 miles from Springer Mount in Georgia to Mount Katahdin in northern Maine. The Appalachian Trail follows the peaks and valleys of the Appalachian Mountains through 14 states. Most of the Appalachian Trail was created where no footpath had existed for people who want to view spectacular scenery and accept the physical challenge of scaling rugged mountains.

Benton MacKaye is often mentioned as the father of the Appalachian Trail. MacKaye offered a proposal in 1921 for a "linear park," a series of recreational communities throughout the Appalachian chain of mountains from New England to Georgia to be connected by a walking trail. His proposal was almost completed by 1937.

Today, the trail passes through national and state parks and forests, game lands and local jurisdictions. Volunteers and hiking club members keep the trails maintained.

ACTIVITY:
Using the pattern sheet, design a patch that people who hike the Appalachian Trail could wear. Consider plants, animals or environmental issues people who hike the Appalachian Trail might encounter. Students could research and discuss things that might be seen on the trail.

An excellent book to share with students is *Blind Courage* by Bill Irwin. The story is about Bill Irwin, who with his seeing-eye dog became the first blind person to hike the 2,168-mile Appalachian Trail.

MATERIALS:
Paper
Scissors
Glue
Crayons
Markers

APPALACHIAN TRAIL PATCH DESIGN

Design and color an Appalachian Trail Patch that hikers on the trail could wear. Consider the different animals, plants or environmental issues that hikers might encounter on the trail. Your patch should include these words "Appalachian Trail." Be creative. When finished, cut out your patch and mount it on cardboard.

GRANDFATHER MOUNTAIN

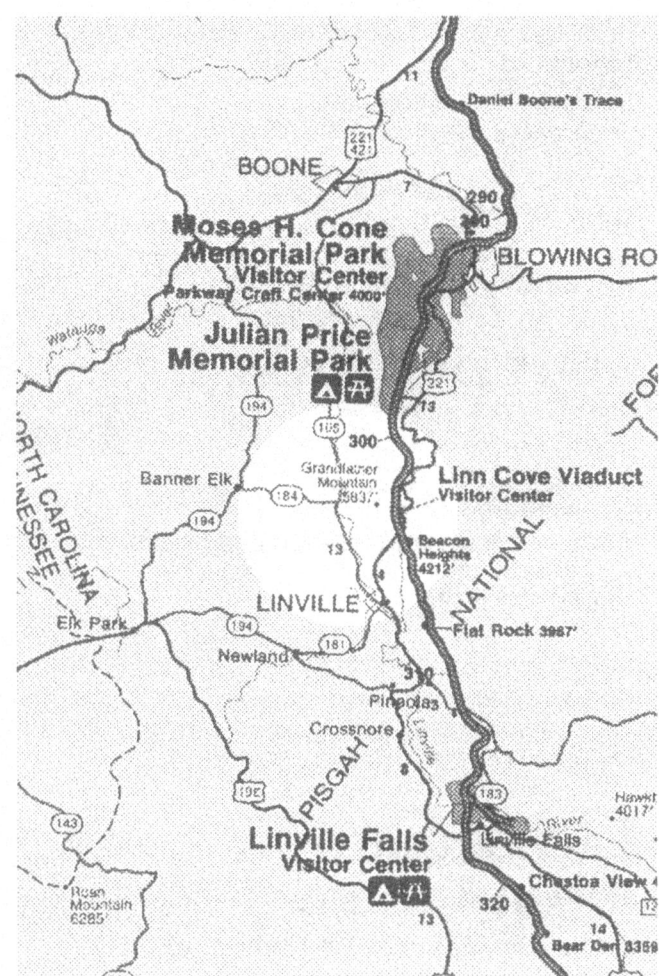

Grandfather Mountain represents the best of the Blue Ridge in rugged strength and grandeur. While the long slopes incline to a sharp, jagged crest line of gray rock, the profile of a grandfather is outlined along the summit. The grandfather face is composed of one of the oldest and most durable rocks known — an ancient quartzite. And the mountain itself is home to more endangered plants and animals than anywhere else in the Southern Appalachians.

Grandfather Mountain, which is privately owned, has dedicated its exceptional ecosystems to the purposes of education and conservation. It is designated as a special conservatory for rare and endangered animals. Your students will get an up-close look at such species as cougar, black bear, and bald and golden eagles. They may also tour the Grandfather Mountain Nature Museum, hike on trails through high-elevation ecosystems, and cross the famous mile-high swinging bridge to ancient rock outcroppings.

Grandfather Mountain is so special that it has been designated as a Biosphere Reserve by the United Nations, which recognizes the great, unique qualities of this mountain. It is home to many research endeavors, ranging from studies on rare and endangered species to the effects of air pollution on high-elevation plants and animals.

Grandfather Mountain is open year round. Schools are asked to schedule their trips by phone (800-468-7325) as far in advance as possible. There is a per person fee for students and adults, with one adult free for every ten children. Grandfather Mountain also provides a theater, coffee shop, picnic area, restrooms, and shuttle buses from the parking area.

The park is easily accessible from U.S. 221 between Linville, NC and the Blue Ridge Parkway. Come prepared for cold weather, rain, winds, and steep terrain. The following activities will hopefully enhance your class trip to this great resource.

WEATHER ON GRANDFATHER MOUNTAIN

GOAL:
Students will recognize the cause and effect of the atmospheric conditions.

The learner will understand how weather predictions are made, recognizing that atmospheric conditions vary in different places and realizing these differences affect the atmospheric conditions.

STATE OBJECTIVES:
STRAND: Science and Math

NORTH CAROLINA
4: The learner will understand and use standard units of metric and customary measure.

4:11: Formulate and solve meaningful problems involving length, weight, time, capacity and temperature and verify reasonableness of answers

TENNESSEE:
Knowing how weather predictions are made

Recognize how atmospheric conditions vary and the effect of changing atmospheric conditions

BACKGROUND INFORMATION:
Students should study the definitions of weather, temperature clouds and precipitation. How do clouds form? How do you predict the weather?

ACTIVITIES:
1. Have students keep a daily log of weather conditions at school and home for a week before this trip. Record the temperature, sky conditions, air conditions, wind direction (make your own weather vane) and wind speeds (use newspapers, television and radio reports to compile information). Compare temperatures at home and school and determine an average. Have a student to research the elevation of your school.

2. When on Grandfather Mountain, have student use the weather instruments on the mountain to collect the weather conditions. After returning to school, have students compare the differences between the two locations and discuss the causes for the differences. Have students take turns as a meteorologist and give the weather forecast.

ISSUES AT GRANDFATHER MOUNTAIN

GOAL:
The learner will understand science ideas by analyzing systems. The learner will use strategies and processes that enhance control of communication skills development.

STATE OBJECTIVES:
NORTH CAROLINA
SCIENCE
- 5.2: Investigate animals and their behavior within natural environments.
- 5.2.1: Compare similarities and differences of animal groups. Engage in activities to explore animal behavior. Compare and contrast various adaptations of different animal groups to their environments.

LANGUAGE ARTS
- 1.1: The learner will apply preparation strategies to comprehend or convey experience and information.
- 2.2: The learner will analyze, synthesize and organize information and discover related ideas, ideas or generalizations.
- 2.3: The learner will apply, extend and expand on information and ideas.
- 3.1: The learner will assess the validity and accuracy of information and ideas.
- 3.2: The learner will detect the value of information and ideas.

TENNESSEE:
SCIENCE:
Realize environmental problems may vary from one community to another.
Identify environmental concerns of the local community.
Realize how individuals affect the environment

LANGUAGE ARTS:
Students will identify correct capitalization and punctuation, write legibly in cursive style and identify relevant and irrelevant information in a paragraph.

PRE-SITE ACTIVITY:
Have students brainstorm questions about animals. To do this, have students prepare two or three questions to ask the guide. Prepare a "What I know, what I want to know, and what I learned" chart.

ON-SITE ACTIVITY:
Discuss issues about the animals living in captivity on Grandfather Mountain such as:

1. Where should the baby animals be placed after being born in captivity? Should they remain with their parents? Is there room for the offspring to live with their parents? Should they be freed in the wild? Should the animals be placed in zoos?

2. Should you feed wild animals? Should visitors be allowed to feed the bears? Do humans contribute to the bears' obesity? Who benefits from feeding the bears?

POST-SITE ACTIVITY:
Have students write a letter to the editor explaining their view on one of these issues. Have students share and discuss these views. Have students prepare a public service announcement that offers a solution. Videotape the ad and share it with other classes. Have students write a response or review of the ads.

SCAVENGER HUNT

BACKGROUND INFORMATION:

Have students as a class brainstorm questions about animals. Have students prepare several questions to ask the guide. Prepare a "What I know, what I want to know, and what I learned" matrix.

STATE OBJECTIVES:

ALL FOR NORTH CAROLINA AND TENNESSEE

ON-SITE ACTIVITY:

1. Scavenger Hunt can be done by individuals or small groups.

2. The Scavenger Hunt questions may be divided or done as a group. If divided into groups, stagger the starting points in the museum. This activity can be done while other classes are doing other activities, such as the swinging bridge, trails, movies or animal habitat.

MATERIALS:

Pencils
Clipboards
Copies of the Scavenger Hunt
Resources: Grandfather Mountain rangers and museum display cases.

SCAVENGER HUNT

BIRDS:

1. Which bird is a bird of prey?
   _____

2. What bird makes the sound of a cat?
   _____

3. Which bird likes to eat fish?
   _____

MINERALS:

1. Is your county represented by a mineral?
   Yes____ No____

2. Which mineral is shaped like a cross?
   _____

TREES:

1. What kind of tree is pictured?
   _____

2. How old is the tree?
   _____

3. Was the tree young or old when man set foot on the moon?
   _____

GOLD:

1. When was gold discovered in North Carolina?
   _____

2. How many gold mines were located on Grandfather Mountain?
   _____

MUSHROOMS:

1. Which mushroom looks like an Easter egg?
   _____

2. List two deadly mushrooms.
   _____

3. Which mushroom looks like a star?
   _____

4. Which mushroom has an odor?
   _____

EDIBLE BERRIES:

1. Which berry could you make tea from?
   _____

2. Which berry is Mildred the Bear's favorite?
   _____

WILDFLOWERS:

1. Which flower has an insect in its name?
   _____

2. Which plant could be used to make tea?
   _____

3. Which flower has a lady's slipper shoe in its name?
   _____

4. Which color would you buy?
   Yellow____ Pink____

5. Is the North Carolina's state flower listed?
   Yes____ No____

6. What is the North Carolina state flower?
   _____

SCAVENGER HUNT

7. Which plant might preach a sermon?
   _____

DEER:

1. What are the antlers covered with?
   _____

2. What are the antlers used for?
   _____

3. What color is the deer at birth?
   _____

4. What color do they turn as winter approaches?
   _____

BLACK BEARS:

1. How much does a cub weigh at birth?
   _____

2. What is the life span of a bear?
   _____

INDIANS:

1. When did Indians last live on Grandfather Mountain?
   _____

2. Which relic was made from clay?
   _____

3. Which relic may have been used as a hammer? (look in Woodland period)
   _____

DANIEL BOONE:

1. What did Daniel Boone search for on Grandfather Mountain?
   _____

2. How long did Daniel Boone live?
   _____

3. Would you carve a message on a tree?
   Yes____ No____

4. Why or why not?
   _____

COUGARS:

1. What are other names for a cougar?
   _____

WEATHER:

1. What is the lowest recorded temperature on Grandfather Mountain?
   _____

2. What is the average winter snowfall?
   _____

3. What is the highest recorded wind speed?
   _____

RARE AND ENDANGERED SPECIES:

1. What does endangered and extinct mean?
   _____

2. How many falcons were released on Grandfather Mountain?
   _____

SCAVENGER HUNT

3. What cave do bats live in?

4. How did Blue Ridge Golden Rod get its name?

5. What do bats use their ears for?

6. What do bats eat?

EAGLES:

1. Why can't the eagles on Grandfather Mountain fly?

2. Which eagle is the national bird?

GEOLOGY:

1. What caused the split rock to split?

2. Which two continents collided?

3. What kind of rock makes up Rough Ridge?

RAVENS:

1. What is the difference between a crow and a raven?

2. Can ravens be taught to talk?

BOTANISTS:

1. Name a famous French botanist.

2. Why was Michaux here?

3. What two Grandfather Mountain plants did Michaux discover?

4. What country was Michaux from?

5. What flower was named for Asa Gray?

AIR POLLUTION:

1. What pollutants form acid rain?

2. What does air pollution do to the forest?

3. What two trees are affected by acid rain?

SPECIAL RECOGNITION:

1. What special recognition has Grandfather Mountain received?

SCAVENGER HUNT ANSWERS

BIRDS:
1. Screech Owl
2. Gray Catbird
3. Kingfisher

MINERALS:
1.
2. Staurolite

TREES:
1.
2.
3.

GOLD:
1.
2.

MUSHROOMS:
1. Caesar's Mushroom
2. Destroying angel and Fly Agaric
3. Earth Star
4. Stinkhorn

EDIBLE BERRIES:
1. Teaberry
2. Blackberries, Huckleberries

WILDFLOWERS:
1. Butterfly Weed
2. Oswego Tea
3. Lady Slipper
4. Subjective
5. Yes. Dogwood
6. Jack-in-the-Pulpit

DEER:
1. Velvet
2. Defense
3. Brown with white spots
4. Grey-brown

BLACK BEARS:
1. Less than a pound
2. 35 years

INDIANS:
1. During the American Revolution
2. The bowl
3. Look in Woodland Period

DANIEL BOONE:
1. Game and Ginseng
2. 1734-1820
3. Subjective

COUGARS:
1. Mountain lion, panther, puma

WEATHER:
1. -32°
2. 57 inches
3. 172.53 m.p.h.

RARE AND ENDANGERED SPECIES:
1.
2. 21
3. Black Rock Cave
4. Blue Ridge Mountains
5.
6.

EAGLES:
1. They have been injured by hunters and part of their wing was removed by a veterinarian.
2. Bald Eagle

GEOLOGY:
1.
2. Africa and North America
3. Sandstone

RAVENS:
1. A raven is larger, a better flyer, more intelligent, noble
2. Yes

BOTANISTS:
1. Andre Michaux
2. To obtain plants for the King's Garden of Versailles
3. Flame Azalea and Red (Catawba) Rhododendron
4. France
5. Gray's Lily

AIR POLLUTION:
1. Ozone, automobiles, trucks, buses, airplanes, industry
2. Use picture to describe
3. Red Spruce and Fraser Fir

SPECIAL RECOGNITION:
1. It has been designated as a Southern Appalachian Biosphere Reserve.

There are four movies available at the park. Topics include the black bear, hawks, cougars and an overview of Grandfather Mountain.

ANIMALS AT GRANDFATHER MOUNTAIN

GOALS:
This is to study the effects of man on the environment and man's effect on endangered and threatened animals, and to compare a private biome (Grandfather Mountain) with state and national biomes.

STATE OBJECTIVES:
NORTH CAROLINA:

2.4: To know that animals adapt to the environment.
2.7: To know that animals are interdependent.
2.7.1: To trace food chains beginning with green plants.

TENNESSEE:

To recognize differences between animals.
To realize that individuals affect the environment.

PRE-SITE ACTIVITY:
Have the students research and discuss the following:

Endangered species
Threatened species
Biome
Private biome
Public biome
Food web
Wildflowers
Trees in the Appalachians

ON-SITE ACTIVITIES:
1. Have students complete the worksheets on the following pages as they tour the site.

2. Have students draw the profile of the mountain as they approach it.

3. Have students speculate on the name of Grandfather Mountain and where it came from.

POST-SITE ACTIVITIES:
1. Have students make food webs.

2. Have students complete the wildflower coloring book.

3. Have students make a wildflower or animal mural.

4. Have students research the Lynn Cove Viaduct, listing the things that make it unusual.

5. Have students research legends of the area.

ANIMALS AT GRANDFATHER MOUNTAIN

COMPLETE THE FOOD WEB FOR THE WHITE-TAILED DEER.
DRAW ARROWS TO CONNECT THE VARIOUS USERS.

ANIMALS AT GRANDFATHER MOUNTAIN

COMPLETE THE FOOD WEB FOR THE BLACK BEAR.
USE ARROWS TO SHOW RELATIONSHIPS.

PLANT HUNT

AS YOU SEE THESE PLANTS, WRITE THE LOCATION.

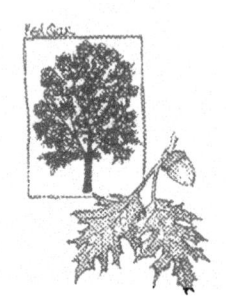

RED OAK

1. _____

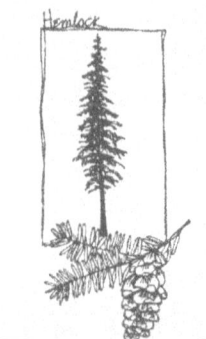

EASTERN HEMLOCK

2. _____

MOUNTAIN LAUREL

3. _____

YELLOW POPULAR

4. _____

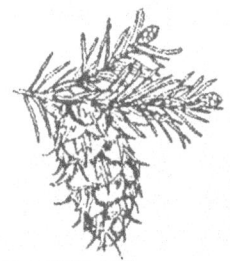

FRASER FIR

5. _____

RHODODENDRON

6. _____

RED MAPLE

7. _____

WHITE PINE

8. _____

RED SPRUCE

9. _____

10. SEDGES _____

ANIMAL WALK

AS YOU HIKE ON THE TRAILS OR WALK THROUGH THE SITE, WRITE THE LOCATION OF EACH ANIMAL YOU SEE ON THE SHEET. WHEN YOU RETURN TO YOUR CLASSROOM, SELECT AN ANIMAL FOR FURTHER STUDY.

PEREGRINE FALCON   BLACK BEAR   RED-TAILED HAWK

1. _____   2. _____   3. _____

GRAY SQUIRREL   COTTONTAIL RABBIT   WHITE-TAILED DEER

4. _____   5. _____   6. _____

FOOD WEB

MAKE YOUR OWN FOOD WEB. WRITE THE NAME OR PICTURE OF THE ANIMAL YOU HAVE CHOSEN AND USE LINES TO SHOW RELATIONSHIPS.

THE WILDFLOWER COLORING BOOK

Anatomy of wild flowers

The Wildflower Coloring Book

Cross-section of wild flower

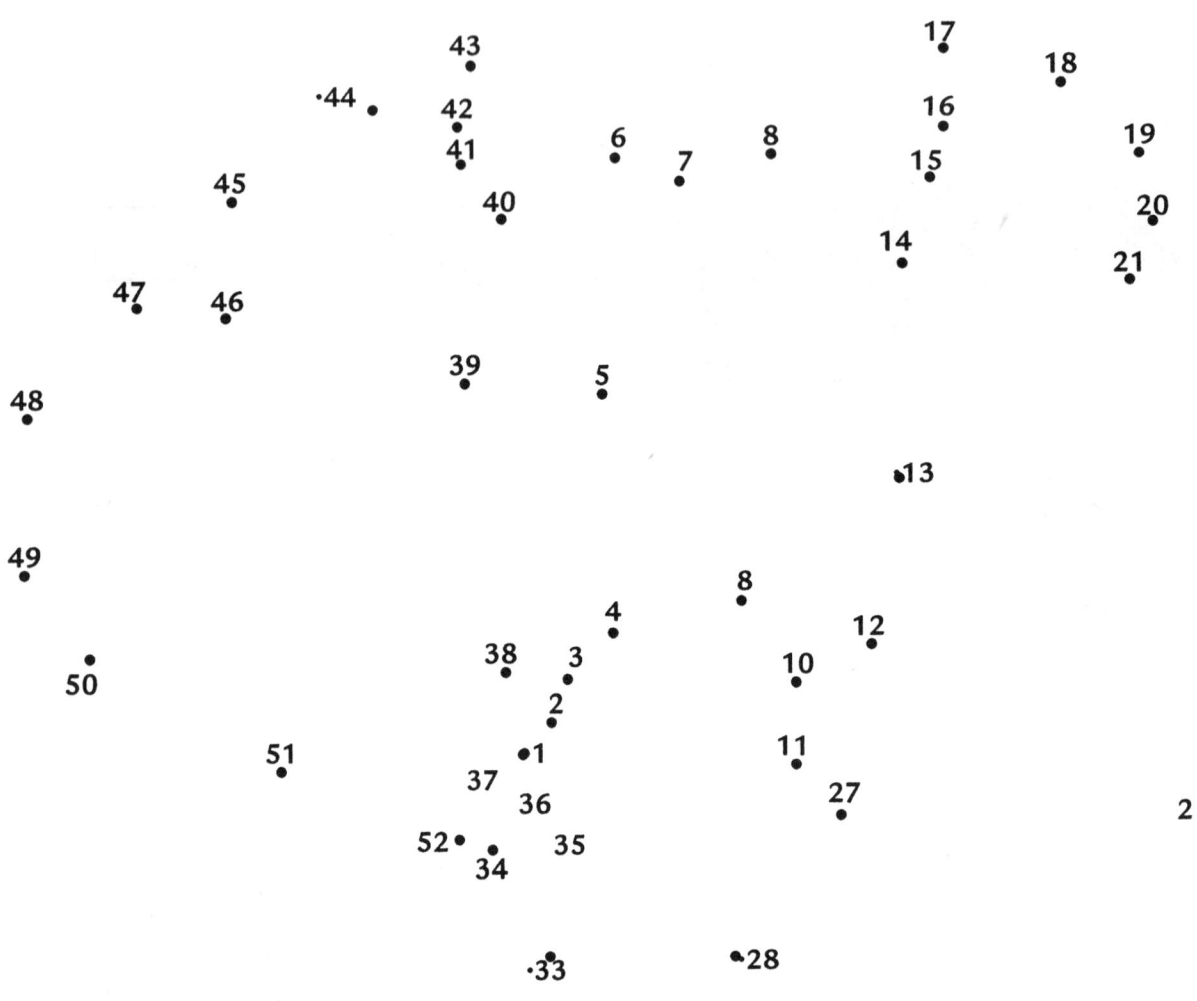

The Wildflower Coloring Book

Yellow Lady's Slipper

Trout Lily

THE WILDFLOWER COLORING BOOK

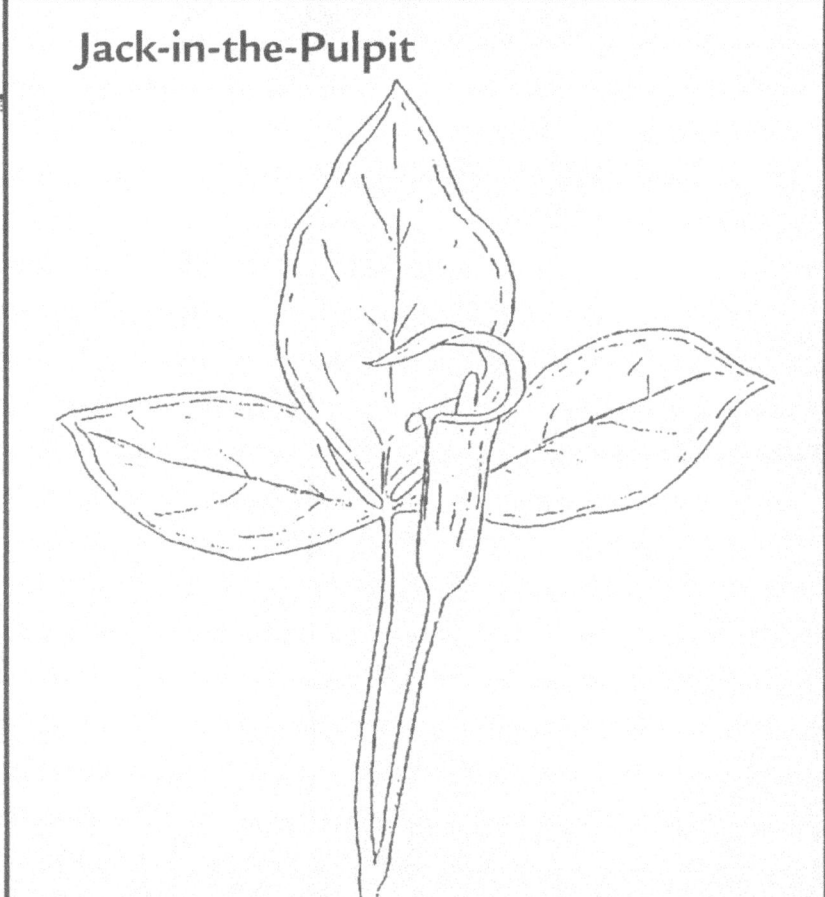

Jack-in-the-Pulpit

THE WILDFLOWER COLORING BOOK

Red Trillium (Wake Robin)

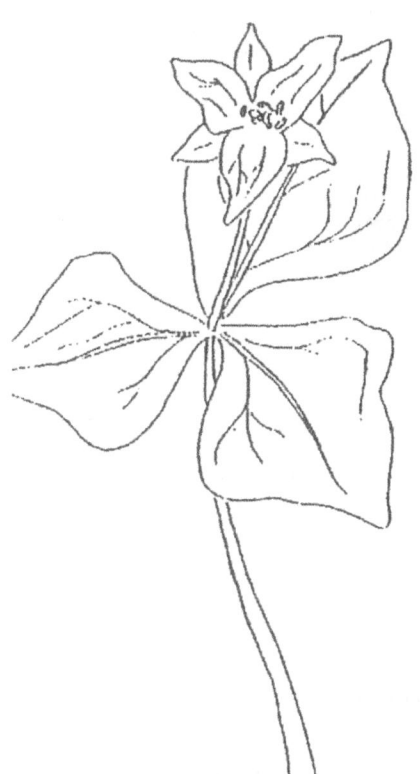

Toadshade (Trillium)

THE WILDFLOWER COLORING BOOK

Wild Geranium

Dutchmen's Britches

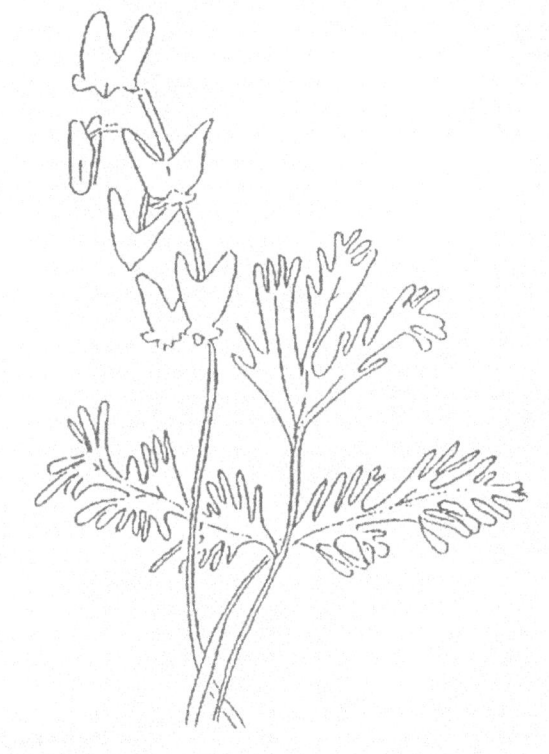

THE WILDFLOWER COLORING BOOK

Violet

Showy Orchid

ANIMAL PUPPETS

GOAL:
The learner will research one of the following animals: black bear, cougar, white-tailed deer, bald eagle or golden eagle. The learner will write a short paragraph about an animal and attach a written paragraph to a paper bag animal puppet they created.

STATE OBJECTIVES:
North Carolina
2: The learner will have a general knowledge of animals.
2.4: The learner will know that animals are adapted to their environment

INTRODUCTION:
Grandfather Mountain provides an excellent habitat for the following animals: black bear, cougar, white-tailed deer, bald eagle and golden eagle. See the attached information sheets for information about each animal.

ACTIVITY:
Using the attached information sheets or using other reference books, have students research one of the animals. Students should find 5-10 facts about their chosen animal and transfer this information into paragraph form on an index card.

Have students construct a puppet of their animal. The index card should be attached to the front of the puppet.

These puppets could be used as a bulletin board display or in a puppet show for younger students.

MATERIALS:
Paper lunch sacks
Construction paper
Glue
Scissors
Yarn
Fake fur
Wiggly eyes
Pipe cleaners
Index cards
Reference books

ANIMAL PUPPETS

AMERICAN BLACK BEAR

Phylum: Chordata

Class: Mammalia

Order: Carnivora

Family: Ursidae

Genus species: Ursus americanus

Geographic range: The distribution of the black bear is mainly in the forested areas of the United States and Canada.

Characteristics and habits: Head and body lengths are five feet to six feet; tail about four inches; and shoulder height is up to three feet. The weight of the black bear is approximately 200 to 600 pounds, females being lighter than males. The most common color phases are black, chocolate brown, and cinnamon brown. A white and blue-black phase are rare.

The usual locomotion is a lumbering walk, but the black bear can be quick if necessary.

Like other bears that sleep through the winter, the black bear becomes fat with the approach of cold weather, finally ceases eating, and goes into a den in a protected location to sleep for the winter.

During hibernation, body temperature drops from 100° F to 88-93° F, the respiration slows, and metabolic rate is depressed. This winter sleep is interrupted by excursions outside during periods of warmer weather. Such outings are more numerous in the southern latitudes. Hibernation usually lasts 3-4 months.

Diet: At least 75% of the black bears' diet consists of vegetable matter, especially fruits, berries, nuts, grass, and roots. The diet also includes insects, fish, rodents, carrion, and occasionally large mammals.

Reproduction: The sexes come together briefly during mating which generally peaks from June to mid-July. Females remain in estrus throughout the season until they mate. They usually give birth every other year, but sometimes wait 3-4 years between litters. Sexual maturity is between three and five years of age. Pregnancy generally lasts 220 days, but there is delayed implantation. The fertilized eggs are not implanted in the uterus until autumn, and embryonic development occurs in the last 10 weeks of pregnancy. Births occur mainly in January and February, commonly while the female is in hibernation. The number of young per litter ranges from 2-5, but usually 2-3. At birth, the young weigh 6-8 pounds and are naked and blind. They are usually weaned at 6-8 months of age, but remain with the mother during their second winter of life. They will leave on their own the next spring.

Life expectancy: About 30-35 years in captivity, 3-5 years in the wild because of its classification as a game species.

COUGAR, PUMA, MOUNTAIN LION, PANTHER

Phylum: Chordata

Class: Mammalia

Family: Felicidae

Genus species: Felis concolor (15 subspecies have been recognized; the rarest is the Florida variety.)

Geographic range: Wilderness areas of western America, from southern Alberta and British Columbia in Canada down to the Straits of Magellan in South America; also isolated populations in the Eastern U.S. and Florida. They may be the widest distributed of all American mammals.

Characteristics: A large, slender cat with small head and long, heavy cylindrical tail and rounded ears that are tufted. Its fur is soft, uniformly dull yellowish-brown, reddish-brown, or gray, paler on the flanks and shoulders and merges into dull whitish on the underparts. Its tail is topped with brown to blackish fur. Total weight is 6 to 8 1/2 feet, or more; its height at the shoulder is 26 to 30 inches. The weight of the male ranges from 100 to 175 pounds. Females weigh about 40 percent less than males. In the tropics, cougars average smaller than in northern and southern extremes of their range.

Habits: This animal lives in a wide range of habitats from deserts to grasslands and rainforests, from sea level to mountain ranges. Each cougar has an extensive territory, through which it roams on a roughly circular path that may be 100 miles in circumference, thus leaving each hunting ground undisturbed for days at a time. Supposedly the strong, silent member of the cat family, the cougar, particularly the male, has been rarely known to yowl in the wild.

Diet: The cougar is a formidable hunter, its prey ranging from small rodents to fully-grown deer. On the average, a North American Cougar may kill one ungulate, such as a White-tailed or mule deer, each week. The prey, usually killed from ambush after dark, is fed upon on the spot, with the remaining carcass dragged to a hiding place and covered with sticks and leaves. The cat may or may not return to feed on its remains. Many cougars learn to make an easier living by preying on domestic livestock, including young horses. This brings the animal in conflict with man, and hunting for the predator is common in the western U.S.

Reproduction: The gestation period is three months, and there are usually two or three young ones in the litter. The cubs are at first heavily marked with black spots that eventually fade. The sexes live a short time together during mating and then go their separate ways again. The young cougars spend up to two years with the mother, learning to hunt and survive on their own.

Life expectancy: Left unmolested by humans, the cougar may live 10-12 years.

History: The earliest modern cats were smallish and made their appearance about 13 million years ago. It took another 10 million years for the big cats (cougar included) to evolve.

GOLDEN EAGLE

Phylum: Chordata

Class: Aves

Order: Falconiformes

Family: Accipitridae

Genus species: Aquila chrysaetos

Geographical range: Lonely mountainous regions of North America, Europe, Northern Asia and Northern Africa. On the East Coast, the golden eagle nests in northern New Hampshire. In winter, some migrate to the Gulf States.

Characteristics: This eagle, larger than most, at 30-40 inches, has a seven-foot wingspan, which allows it soar very gracefully. Young birds have scattered white markings, and adults have dark-brown bodies, with the top of the head and the neck golden brown. The legs of this bird, unlike the bald eagle, have feathers down to their toes. The bill is large and strong; the upper half curves down sharply over the lower. Strong toes and sharp talons grasp prey.

Habits: The Golden Eagle usually nests on rocky ledges on steep mountain sides, although occasionally nests are in tall trees. The nests are very large, with one reported to be seven feet high and six feet across. The Golden Eagle usually mates for life, and frequently returns yearly to the same nesting area, usually to the same nest. Both parents are responsibly for warming the eggs of their brood, guarding the nest, and bringing food to the young.

Diet: Golden eagles feed on mammals, such as rabbits and fawns and sometimes young lamb. They also catch a variety of birds, including waterfowl.

Reproduction: The eagle has one brood a year. Usually 2 or 3 eggs are laid at one time and incubate for 34-35 days. At 10-13 weeks, the eaglets are ready to leave the nest.

History: In Western North America the golden eagle has the name "war eagle" because Native Americans preferred its wing and tail feathers for war bonnets.

Life expectancy: 30 years

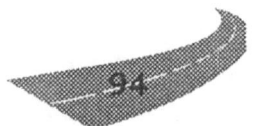

ANIMAL PUPPETS

WHITE-TAILED DEER

Phylum: Chordata

Class: Mammalia

Order: Artiodactyla

Family: Cervidae

Genus species: Odocoileus virginia

Geographic range: This species occurs over most of North and Central America and parts of South America.

Characteristics: A large buck or male may weigh 200-300 pounds and may measure up to seven feet from the head to the tip of the one-foot tail, and stands about 34 inches at the withers. They have limber but compact bodies. The ears are large but usually slender. The legs are long and slender and have paired hooves. Generally their fur is reddish-brown or gray above, with white undersides and a white tail.

The general form of the antler is characteristic in males of various species. They have solid, bony outgrowths arising from the frontal bones and with this species have one main beam with side tines (spikes). Antlers grow up to 30 inches long with the end tines pointing upward. The antlers are shed and produced anew each year.

In the White-tailed deer, the upper incisors are usually absent or poorly developed, and a gall bladder is usually absent. They have prominent facial glands below each eye, and their senses of sight, hearing, and smell are very acute.

Habits: Deer like most browsing animals are crepuscular. Most live in small bands comprising family groups. Although males are prone to be solitary seasonally, they are known to be polygamous, collecting harems and battling other bucks for possession of the does. During the rutting (mating) season, they are likely to be unpredictable and may attack with either antlers or hooves. The underside of the tail is white and forms a conspicuous flag when the tail is raised, as in cases of alarm. It is a strong swimmer, capable of making excellent speed in the water, as well as running as fast as 30 mph on land and jumping as high as 8 feet.

Diet: In the wild, White-tailed deer feed mainly on twigs and leaves rather than on grass, and also on nuts and acorns. It often starves in winter.

Reproduction: Breeding takes place in late autumn and after a gestation period of 215-230 days, the doe produces from one to four young precocial, called fawns. They are weaned after about four months, and a doe can breed by the age of two. Their life expectancy is 9-12 years.

Hunting: White-tailed along with Mule and Black-tailed deer are the most widely hunted big game animal in the U.S., and are second only to rabbit as the most-hunted mammal world-wide. The flesh, or venison, of most deer is esteemed as food. In certain areas deer have occasionally become overabundant, and because of the depletion of natural predators such as coyotes, wolves, wild cats, and bears, disease and starvation often decimate local populations. Now, however, checked hunters, and flexible game regulations tend to control their numbers.

ANIMAL PUPPETS

BALD EAGLE

Phylum:	Chordata
Class:	Aves
Order:	Falconiformes
Family:	Accipitridae

Genus species: Haliaeetus leucocephala

Geographic range: Being one of the sea eagles, the bald eagles nests along fresh or salt waters in North America, most of the U.S. and south into Mexico.

Characteristics: The adult is blackish brown with a snow white head and tail, which is visible in its fourth year. It has unfeathered strong feet and toes with sharp talons, stout legs, and a strongly hooked bill that is nearly as long as its head. Adults are usually 30-40 inches long with a wingspan of 6-8 feet, with the female being larger than the male (usually by 1/3). Their eyes are highly developed, and its vision binocular (capable of altering focus from two feet to two miles and still see sharply) and 3 to 8 times keener than the eyes of a man.

Habits: Diurnal bird of prey. Kills with its talons and dismembers with its bill. Will sit perched on a tree limb for hours, seeming not to move or blink.

Diet: Feeds on fish, mammals, and reptiles. Although main diet is fish, it catches very few itself, either pirating from other birds such as ospreys or picking up dead fish on the shore.

Reproduction: The breeding season is early spring (Florida in October, southern states in December, central states in January, and Maine/Canada in mid-March). They have the same mates for life and return to the same nest every year. The nest is a huge, bulky structure of sticks lined with grass or moss, usually built on a cliff or pinnacle of rock within easy flight of sea, lake, or stream. The nest has 4 to 12 inches added to it each year. The female lays 1 to 3 eggs; 35 to 40 days later they hatch (it takes the baby about 24 hours to break itself free of its shell), with both parents sharing the incubation and care of the young. The eaglets eat more than their own weight every day. The grey down is replaced by dark brown juvenile plumage in about eight weeks, with adult plumage taking 5-10 years. The young stay with the adults until they learn how to hunt and kill.

Conservation: The Bald Eagle is on the federal endangered species list. It has become scarce in the lower 48 states because of pesticide poisoning which causes infertility and fragile eggshells. The 1970 overall population was slightly more than 1000. As a result of the DDT ban and repopulation techniques, the number increased to 5000 by 1982. (Numbers do not include Alaska's population of bald eagles, presently estimated at 11,000).

History: Because of its fish-eating habits, the Bald Eagle was considered an enemy of Alaskan salmon fisheries. Alaska was one of the last states to halt the bounty on eagle carcasses in 1952. Between 1917-1952, Alaskans killed and paid for 102,946 of these birds. The Bald Eagle is the emblem of the United States.

GRANDFATHER MOUNTAIN WILDLIFE HABITAT

GOAL:
Students will define habitat and describe elements of habitats in order to design an appropriate habitat for an animal.

STATE OBJECTIVES:
NORTH CAROLINA
SCIENCE
2: The learner will have a general knowledge of animals.
2.4: Know that animals are adapted to their environment.
2.7: Know that animals are independent.
2.7.5: Discuss how humans must care for the environment to ensure that animals remain healthy and species survive.

BACKGROUND INFORMATION:
Habitat includes food, shelter and water that an animal needs to survive and reproduce. It can also be the environment where an organism lives.

Each species of wildlife has specific habitat requirements and is limited by the quality and quantity of available habitat. The plants and surface water which compose habitats are influenced by temperature, rainfall, sunlight and the human activity. Habitats often change as a result of human disturbances or natural occurrences. These changes can be as drastic as a mining operation or as subtle as a decaying oak tree. These changes force animals to adapt, compete with others in the habitat, or die.

As the environment recovers, whether using natural plant succession or human assistance, new plants grow. This newly-created habitat often favors species not present before the environment was disturbed, which allows wildlife managers to manipulate habitats to meet the needs of a certain species.

LITERATURE CONNECTION:
MacMillan/McGraw-Hill. Grade Five. *Don't Forget to Fly Story — Tonweya and the Eagles*

Some people say Grandfather Mountain received its name because it has the shape of an old man's face as he is lying down. Have students write a tall tale explaining how Grandfather Mountain got its name. If it reminds you of an old man's face, why did the old man lie down? Whose grandfather was he? Was he a giant? Who carved the mountain this way?

MATERIALS:
Teacher's Guide to Grandfather Mountain
Reference resources
Poster board/large drawing paper
Colored tiles
Drawing/coloring implements

PRE-SITE ACTIVITY:
At Grandfather Mountain there are black bears, white-tailed deer, Western cougars, bald eagles and golden eagles. Although these share Grandfather Mountain, each has unique habitat needs and resources.

Have the students research one of these animals, focusing on its habitat needs and the way the animal has adapted to its environment. What are its food, shelter, reproductive and survival needs and techniques?

ON-SITE ACTIVITIES:
Have the students concentrate on the way Grandfather Mountain attempts to meet the needs of this animal. Have students describe the habitat. What is done to allow the animal to live naturally? What problems are in a captive habitat? How are these problems be corrected? Make a list of necessities for the habitat and a list of things which would be nice to have. Describe how these needs would be fulfilled — place, people, money etc.

POST-SITE ACTIVITIES:
Have students design a habitat for their animal, including must necessities and niceties.

Using colored tiles and poster board, have students draw the habitat to scale and then fill in water, shelter, food sources, etc. This may be completed in several dimensions.

Upon completing the habitat, have students write a report from the animal's viewpoint-of view describing its way of life.

GRANDFATHER MOUNTIAN CROSSWORD PUZZLE

```
R Z O P S S W I N G I N G B R I D G E L
R E E D L I A T E T I H W G B U A C N O
K R I E B O T U E L G A E D L A B Z K R
E E J Q N V M W E S T E R N C O U G A R
N H R X V G D O I B Y O Q N I I Y I R T
D T F E G O L D E N E A G L E W P Z P H
A A T U E Q U Z D E N E T A E R H T V A
N F A I T R Q C R H J B Y D F V Q Z Y B
G D Z W X I T Q M K O L J R F H B H Q I
E N E I S F T S Y S I S B J X T X E W T
R A D R L U C Q A O M X P V O H O I K A
E R H A J U N B S M G O M E J D C F L T
D G E E Y Y I H K O T M U U C U H R T I
H E R B S P T Y Z U A S X N S I Y C I S
H H O K H R X W Y N I L I O T E E Z N B
G E S C R E E Z W Z H I B R Q A U S E D
X K I A G V H F P N B A D X H S I M R H
W A O L A G U F U M G R Z W N C R N M O
K D N B T F R M V T T T C R L O R R T M
L L O R T N O C L A C I G O L O I B R G
```

BALDEAGLE

BLACKBEAR

EROSION

GRANDFATHER

MUSEUM

SWINGINGBRIDGE

WESTERNCOUGAR

BIOLOGICALCONTROL

CHRISTMASTREE

EXTINCT

HABITAY

SOIL

THREATENED

WHITETAILDEER

BIRCH

ENDANGERED

GOLDENEAGLE

MOUNTAIN

SPECIES

TRAIL

GRANDFATHER CROSSWORD ANSWERS

```
. . . . . S W I N G I N G B R I D G E .
R E E D L I A T E T I H W . . . . . . .
. R . . . . . E L G A E D L A B . . . .
E E . . . . . W E S T E R N C O U G A R
N H . . . . . . . . . . . . . . . . . .
D T . E G O L D E N E A G L E . . . . H
A A . . E . . . D E N E T A E R H T . A
N F . . R . . . . . . . . . . . . . . B
G D . . . T . . L . . . . . . . . . . I
E N . . . T S . . I S . . . . . . . . T
R A . R . C . A O M . P . . H . . . . A
E R . A . N . S M . O M E . . C . . T
D G E E . . I . . T . U U C . . R . . .
. . R B . T . . . S . N S I . . I . .
. . O K . . X . . . L I . T E E . . B
. . S C . E . . . I . R . A U S . . .
. . I A . . . . . . A . . H . I M . .
. . O L . . . . . . R . . C . N . .
. . N B . . . . . . T . . . . . . .
. L O R T N O C L A C I G O L O I B . .
```

WORD LIST

BALDEAGLE
BLACKBEAR
EROSION
GRANDFATHER
MUSEUM
SWINGINGBRIDGE
WESTERNCOUGAR

BIOLOGICALCONTROL
CHRISTMASTREE
EXTINCT
HABITAT
SOIL
THREATENED
WHITETAILDEER

BIRCH
ENDANGERED
GOLDENEAGLE
MOUNTAIN
SPECIES
TRAIL

_____   _____   _____   _____   _____
_____   _____   _____   _____   _____
_____   _____   _____   _____   _____

MUSEUM SCAVENGER HUNT II

1. Where can the white-tailed deer be found in our country?

2. Is there a threat of extinction for the white-tailed deer?

3. What color is the white-tailed deer's coat during the summer? During winter?

4. What are three other names for the cougar?

5. What is the food for cougars in the wild?

6. Which type of cougar is more plentiful — the Eastern cougar or Western cougar? Explain.

7. Explain the bodily process of hibernation.

8. What is the normal diet of a black bear?

9. What is the life expectancy of a black bear?

10. What does the word "raven" mean to the Cherokee?

11. What is the difference between a raven and a crow?

12. When can a raven be seen at Grandfather Mountain?

13. When did the eagle become an emblem of the U.S.?

14. Which bird (the bald eagle or golden eagle) inhabits mountainous or hilly terrain?

15. Which type of rock begins as mud?

16. Which rock began as gravel deposited in a river bed?

17. How old are the oldest rocks on Grandfather Mountain?

18. How did the split in "Split Rock" develop?

19. When was gold was discovered in North Carolina?

20. How much does the largest gold nugget on display in North Carolina weigh?

21. What is secondary or alluvial gold?

22. What does the scientific compound name $Be_3 Al_2 O_{18}$ mean?

23. What are five types of quartz found in North Carolina?

24. What color is Kyanite?

25. What mushroom could be a member of the legal profession?

26. What are the two poisonous mushrooms on display?

27. What is an example of a "cosmic" mushroom?

MUSEUM SCAVENGER HUNT II

28. What is the study of plants called?

29. Who discovered and named the plants on Grandfather Mountain? When? What country was he from?

30. Why did this botanist come to North America?

31. What two plants did he discover?

32. What rare plant named after another famous botanist blooms on Grandfather Mountain on high grassy areas during June and July?

33. What type of wildflower blooms only in September?

34. Which wildflower resembles a lady's shoe?

35. Which wildflower name reminds you of Tennessee's state flower?

36. Which wildflower should always be remembered?

37. What type of endangered plant is considered to be the most beautiful on Grandfather Mountain?

38. Which owl is native to North Carolina?

39. Which bat can only be found in North Carolina on Grandfather Mountain?

40. What species of goldenrod was federally listed as threatened?

41. Which plant was discovered and named by the French botanist Andre Michaeux?

42. What type of rare squirrel can be found on Grandfather Mountain?

43. What are two types of dying trees on Grandfather Mountain?

44. What are three reasons why these trees are dying?

45. What are two sources of air pollution that affect Grandfather Mountain?

46. What is the highest peak in Eastern America?

47. When do scientists believe the sequence of rock building on Grandfather Mountain began?

48. Which trail did you hike today?

49. What is the Indian word for Grandfather Mountain that also means "great winged one"?

50. Which type of wildflower is named for an Indian smoking device?

MUSEUM SCAVENGER HUNT II

1. All over the U.S. except for a small portion of the West
2. No, the population today is at its largest.
3. In summer it is reddish-brown; in winter it is heavier grey-brown
4. mountain lion, panther, puma
5. deer
6. Western cougar. There are only 20 Eastern cougars in the Everglades.
7. Because winter brings a shortage of food, the bear's bodily processes slow down, resulting in hibernation. During hibernation, the black bear breathes once every 45 seconds, and the heart beats eight beats a minute.
8. Considered a carnivore, the black bear is really more of a vegetarian. The black bear eats grass, leaves, berries, acorns, nuts and insects.
9. The life expectancy of a bear is up to 35 years.
10. Raven means "great war chief."
11. Raven is larger, a better flyer and shows more intelligence.
12. year-round
13. In 1789 when George Washington took office.
14. Golden eagle. The bald eagle is a water bird.
15. phyllite
16. metaconglomerate
17. 1 billion years
18. The split began as a small fracture when earth stresses acted on the rock to break it. Ice froze in the joint, separating the rock further.
19. 1799
20. 13.9 oz
21. Gold freed from original rock by weathering processes and found in river or stream beds.
22. Beryl with emerald
23. mud inclusion, rock crystal, amethyst, smoky amethyst, champagne
24. blue
25. Lawyer's wig or shaggy mane (coprinus comatus)
26. destroying angel or fly-agaric
27. earth star
28. botany
29. Andre Michaeux, 1794, France
30. He came to gather plants for the royal gardens at the palace at Versailles.
31. Flame azalea rhododendron, red rhododendron, Michaeux's lily
32. Gray's lily
33. Closed Gentian
34. Pink Lady's Slipper
35. Iris cristata
36. Forget-me-not
37. Heller's Blazing Star
38. Eastern screech owl — red phase
39. Virginia big-eared bat
40. Blue Ridge Golden rod
41. Appalachian aven or spreading aven
42. northern flying squirrel
43. Red spruce and Fraser fir
44. wooly aphids (insects), acid rain and air pollution
45. Automobiles, buses, airplanes, oil and coal powered plants, industrial boilers
46. Mount Mitchell at 6,684 feet
47. more than one billion years ago
48. Black Rock hiking trail
49. Tanawa
50. Indian pipes

HABITATS ON GRANDFATHER MOUNTAIN

Name: _____

BLACK BEAR:

1. What are five things black bears eat?
   _____

2. How much do black bears weigh?
   _____

3. How tall are black bears?
   _____

4. What colors are black bears?
   _____

5. How fast can a black bear run?
   _____

6. What is the body temperature of a black bear during hibernation?
   _____

7. When do black bears mate?
   _____

8. When are cubs born?
   _____

9. How many cubs are usually born to the mother?
   _____

10. How often do black bears deliver cubs?
    _____

11. What are cubs like at birth?
    _____

12. How long do cubs usually stay with their mother?
    _____

13. How long do black bears usually live?
    _____

COUGARS:

14. What else are cougars called?
    _____

15. What do cougars look like?
    _____

16. How large are cougars?
    _____

17. How far can cougars roam?
    _____

18. What do cougars eat?
    _____

19. How many cubs are usually born to a mother?
    _____

20. What do newborn cougar cubs look like?
    _____

21. How long do cougar cubs stay with their mother?
    _____

22. How long do cougares usually live?
    _____

WHITE-TAILED DEER

23. Where do white-tailed deer live?
    _____

24. In what types of groups do deer live?
    _____

25. How much do deer weigh?
    _____

26. What does the white-tail deer look like:
    _____

ANIMAL HABITATS ON GRANDFATHER MOUNTAIN

27. When a deer senses danger, what does it do with its tail?

28. How long are the male's antlers?

29. How long do males keep their antlers?

30. How many fawn are born to each doe?

31. How do fawns keep safe while their mothers hunt for food?

32. What do white-tail deer eat?

BALD EAGLES AND GOLDEN EAGLES

33. Where do bald eagles nest?

34. What do bald eagles eat?

35. How do they get their food?

36. What does a bald eagle look like?

37. What is the wingspan of the bald eagle?

38. Where does the golden eagle usually live?

39. What is the wingspan of the golden eagle?

40. Where does the golden eagle nest?

41. What does the golden eagle eat?

42. What does the the adult golden eagle look like?

43. What is the main difference in the feathers of the golden and bald eagle?

44. How far can an eagle see?

45. How many eggs do eagles usually lay?

46. How long does it take for the eggs to hatch?

47. Who takes care of the baby eagles?

48. When do baby eagles learn to fly?

49. How long do baby eagles stay with their parents?

50. Is it legal to hunt eagles?

ANIMAL HABITATS ON GRANDFATHER MOUNTAIN

ANIMAL HABITAT ANSWER SHEET

1. vegetables, fruit, berries, nuts, roots, insects, fish, rodents, carrion
2. 200-600 pounds
3. 5-6 feet tall (from head to tail), stands 3 feet at the shoulder
4. black, chocolate brown, cinnamon brown
5. up to 30 m.p.h.
6. body temperature drops to 88° to 93° F from 100° F
7. June and early July
8. January and February
9. 2 to 5 cubs per litter
10. usually every other year
11. cubs weigh 6-8 oz. at birth, and they are blind and naked
12. usually weaned at 6-8 months, but stay with their mother until the following spring
13. 25-30 years
14. mountain lion or panther
15. large, slender, yellowish-brown cat, white muzzle and eyebrows, dark black line around eyes
16. 6-8.5 feet in length, stands 2-2.5 feet at shoulder
17. as much as 100 miles in a circular pattern
18. rodents, deer, fish
19. 2 or 3 cubs
20. blue eyes, heavy black spots that eventually fade
21. 2 years
22. 10-12 years
23. North and Central America, parts of South America
24. in small bands — a family group
25. 200-300 pounds
26. reddish-brown fur with a white underside, distinctive white tail
27. raises like a flag
28. up to 30 inches long
29. they grow new antlers each year.
30. 1-4 fawns
31. they hide in the forest and stay perfectly still.
32. twigs, leaves and acorns
33. along freshwater or saltwater in North America
34. fish
35. they rob other birds or pick up dead fish on the shore
36. the adult is blackish-brown with a snow-white head and tail
37. 2.5-3 feet
38. lonely mountainous regions of North America, Europe, Northern Asia and North Africa
39. 7 feet
40. rocky ledges, steep mountain sides
41. small animals, like rabbits and young deer
42. dark-brown bodies with a golden-brown head and neck
43. golden eagle has feathers down to its toes.
44. 2 to 4 miles
45. 1 to 3 eggs
46. 35 to 40 days
47. both the mother and father
48. after about 8 weeks
49. until they learn to hunt
50. no

FROM ONE TEACHER TO ANOTHER ...

ANIMAL HABITAT AND WILDLIFE EXHIBIT:

1. Students may purchase food to feed animals.

2. If students buy wildflowers, put their name on their bag and leave it at the wildflower booth. Pick them up before leaving.

MUSEUM:

1. Pass out a museum scavenger hunt to each child. Children may work together to find answers, but each child needs to fill in their own form.

2. Students should use clipboards.

3. Group leaders collect the forms to be graded and returned next week. Prizes will be awarded for highest scores.

SWINGING BRIDGE AND GIFT SHOP:

1. Adults must be at the beginning, middle and end of the bridge.

2. Students should cross the bridge in small groups and one at a time.

3. Students are not allowed to go beyond the end of the bridge to the rock formation. Crossing the bridge is the students' decision.

4. Remind the students to watch out for hats and glasses falling off while on the bridge.

5. At the gift shop/snack bar, students may purchase souvenirs. NO KNIVES or any item resembling a weapon may be purchased.

6. This is a good spot for a restroom break.

7. While at the gift shop, the group needs to stop at the weather station and record the following on the group leader's card: time, date, temperature and speed in knots and miles per hour.

BLACK ROCK HIKING TRAIL:

1. Students must stay behind the group leader.

2. Students must stay on the trails and walk.

3. Students should not pick wildflowers.

4. Keep litter in backpacks.

5. Each student is responsible for recording information from numbered post on the trail. Students should record their information and number on an index card.

6. Stop at #30. A teacher will be stationed on the rock formation. Five or six students at a time will be allowed on the formation.

DIRECTIONS TO GRANDFATHER MOUNTAIN FROM JOHNSON CITY, TN:

1. Leave Johnson City.

2. Travel on Hwy. 181 South to intersection for Elizabethton.

3. Follow Hwy. 321 (Hwy. 67) through Elizabethton to Hampton.

4. Continue on Hwy. 19E South past Elk Park to Cranberry.

5. At Cranberry, follow Hwy. 194 to Newland.

6. In Newland, turn left on Hwy. 181 South toward Linville.

7. In Linville, continue straight on Hwy. 221.

8. Stop at the Grandfather Mountain entrance gate to get tickets.

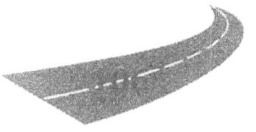

HISTORY OF GRANDFATHER MOUNTAIN

Name: _____

Date: _____

1. When was the mountain was created? _____
2. How was the mountain was formed? _____
3. How old are the oldest rock formations on Grandfather Mountain? _____
4. What was the original Indian name for the mountain? What did the name mean? _____
5. Who named the mountain Grandfather? Why? _____
6. On which hiking trail can you best see the outline of Grandfather's face? _____
7. What is the highest peak in the Blue Ridge Mountains? What is the elevation? _____

MATCHING

_____ Asa Gray A. Highest peak in the Black Mountains

_____ Andre Michaux B. French botanist who climbed Grandfather Mt. in 1794 while on an expedition for King Louis XVI

_____ Mount Mitchell C. Highest peak in Unaka Mountains

_____ Hugh Mac Rae Morton D. Early explorer who hunted in Grandfather Mt. in the 1760's.

_____ Roan Mountain E. Inherited Grandfather Mountain from his grandfather in 1932. Built the Mile-High Swinging Bridge.

_____ Daniel Boone F. Discovered rare lily that blooms on Grandfather Mountain in June and July.

ANSWERS

1. 620 million years ago
2. Two of the earth's plates slammed together, thrusting great sections of the continent upward.
3. 1.05 billion years
4. Tanawha—fabulous hawk or eagle
5. Pioneers (looks like an old man's face on one of the cliffs)
6. Profile Trail
7. Grandfather Mountain's Calloway Park (5,964 ft.)

MATCHING

F Asa Gray
B Andre Michaux
A Mount Mitchell
E Hugh Mac Rae Morton
C Roan Mountain
D Daniel Boone

MY GRANDFATHER MOUNTAIN PLANT

NAME: _____

DATE DUE: _____

The plant/tree I am responsible for learning about is:
_____

What I found out about my plant/tree:
_____
_____
_____
_____

Picture of my plant/tree:

WILDFLOWER QUILT

NAME: _____

DATE DUE: _____

My wildflower:

_____

Information about my wildflower:

_____

_____

_____

_____

1. Draw a picture of your wildflower on the quilt square.
2. Write the name of your flower on the quilt square.
3. Write at least two facts about your wildflower on the square.
4. Make your squares colorful and neat.

SUGGESTED GROUP ACTIVITY SCHEDULE

ARRIVE: 10-10:30 a.m.

GROUPS: There will be four groups. Two groups will begin at habitat/museum/wildflower area while the other two groups will begin at Black Rock Trail/Bridge area. These groups will exchange areas in the afternoon.

LUNCH: Groups will eat lunch in the covered shelter by the museum or in the room at the bridge between 11:30 a.m. and 1:00 p.m.

GROUP SCHEDULES:

	GROUP I	GROUP II	GROUP III	GROUP IV
10:30	habitat	museum	movie hike	lunch bridge
11:30	museum	movie	animal habitat	to hike
12:00	bridge	lunch		
12:30	lunch	lunch		
1:00	to hike	to bridge	animal habitat/museum	movie
2:00	to hike	museum	movie habitat	animal habitat
2:30	to bridge			
3:30	In theater	In theater	In theater	In theater
4:00	Leave for School	Leave for School	Leave for School	Leave for School

GRANDFATHER MOUNTAIN WEATHER STATION

BACKGROUND INFORMATION:

We have used data from Fairmont Elementary School in Johnson City, TN. You will want to substitute data from your own site.

TEMPERATURE

FAIRMONT		GRANDFATHER MT.	
9:00 a.m.	63°	12:45 p.m.	54.6°
10:30 a.m.	65°	1:10 p.m.	54.1°
11:30 a.m.	70°	2:45 p.m.	54.3°
12:15 p.m.	73°	3:00 p.m.	54.3°
1:30 p.m.	76°		
2:30 p.m.	78°		

WIND SPEED

FAIRMONT	GRANDFATHER MT.	
calm	12:45 p.m.	15 knots NE
	1:10 p.m.	15 knots NE
	2:45 p.m.	15 knots NE
	3:00 p.m.	20 knots NE

1 knot = 1.15 mph

SNOWFALL

MONTH	INCHES
October	1.0
November	3.0
December	24.5
January	16.5
February	1.0
March	5.5
April	0.0

ACTIVITY:

Use the collected data to complete the following problems.

1. Make a double line graph to chart the temperature at Fairmont and Grandfather Mountain.

2. Convert the wind speed to miles per hour.

3. Find the difference between the temperatures for Fairmont at 2:30 p.m. and Grandfather Mountain for 3:00 p.m. What factors would make the difference? What general rule about these factors could you make?

4. The elevation of Johnson City is approximately 1,200 feet above sea level. At the swinging bridge elevation is 5,305 feet above sea level. What is the difference?

5. Write a number sentence to show how far you hiked on Black Rock Trail.

6. The distance from Johnson City to the entrance to Grandfather Mountain Biosphere Reservation is 49.8 miles. It is another two miles to the museum and habitat area. Traveling from the museum parking lot to the Black Rock hiking trail is 1.2 miles. From Black Rock hiking trail to the Swinging Bridge is 0.3 mile. Calculate the total distance traveled by bus during the trip to Grandfather Mountain.

7. A mile equals 5,280 feet. The elevation at the bridge was 5,305 feet. How much above a mile is the bridge?

8. The altitude or elevation at the bridge is 5,305 feet. The height at the museum is 4,720 and at the entrance gate is 4,270 feet. Is the elevation greater between the bridge and the museum, or the museum and the gate entrance?

9. Create a bar graph showing the monthly snowfall on Grandfather Mountain using the provided data.

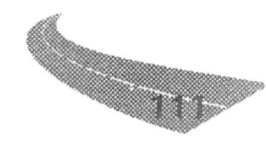

GRANDFATHER MOUNTAIN INFORMATION SHEET

WHEN: Friday, October 13, 1995

TIME: 8:30 a.m. to 5:30 p.m.

COST: $15.00 per student (transportation and admission fee)

$10.00 per parent chaperone

DUE BY: Thursday, October 5, 1995

WHAT TO BRING:

Jacket (a must!)
Head covering
Rain gear (depending on weather)
Sturdy, comfortable shoes (no sandals or slick bottoms)
Safe, sensible clothing (layers are best)
Sack lunch with two drinks
Backpack (to hold lunch, notebooks, etc.)
Clipboard
Spiral notebook
Pencils
Camera (optional)
Money for gift shop/snacks (optional)

ACTIVITIES:

Nature hike (approx. 1 mile on Black Rock Trail)
Visitation of animal habitats
Wildflower exhibit
Nature movie
Swinging bridge excursion
Museum scavenger hunt

_____ I am interested in chaperoning.

_____ I am interested in sponsoring a child.

Name: _____   Student's homeroom: _____

CHAPERONE EVALUATION

TO: GRANDFATHER MOUNTAIN CHAPERONES

FROM: 5TH GRADE TEACHERS

RE: TRIP EVALUATION

We wish to express thanks those who volunteered to chaperone our Grandfather Mountain trip. Your presence supports the importance of the students' learning.

We ask that you continue to help us by completing the following evaluation form.

1. **Transportation:**   Poor   Adequate   Good
   Comments:

2. **Preparation of Chaperones:**   Inadequate   Helpful   Very Helpful
   Comments:

3. **Preparation of Students:**   Inadequate   Helpful   Very Helpful
   Comments:

4. **Activities:**

Habitat:	Routine	Interesting	Challenging
Wildflowers:	Routine	Interesting	Challenging
Museum:	Routine	Interesting	Challenging
Trail:	Routine	Interesting	Challenging
Bridge:	Routine	Interesting	Challenging

5. What was the best part of the trip?

6. What was the least effective part of the trip? Why?

7. Was the cost of the trip appropriate?

8. Suggestions for improvements:

MOUNT MITCHELL

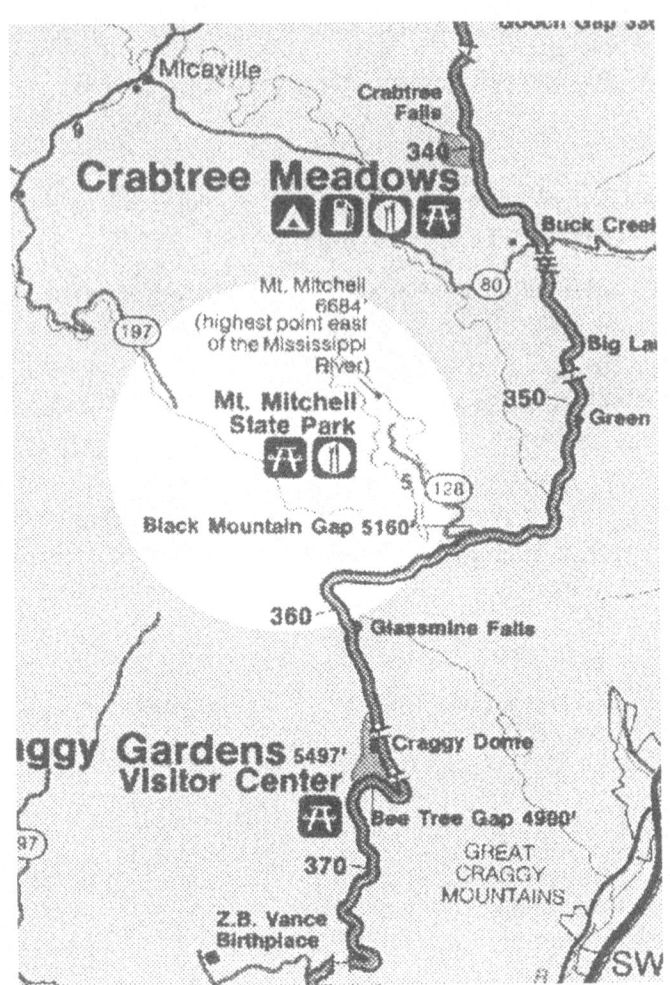

Mt. Mitchell, the central dome on the Black Mountain Ridge, is noted for being the highest mountain in the eastern United States, at 6,684 feet. But it also boasts a rich natural and cultural history and is an excellent setting for a school field trip.

In 1835, Dr. Elisha Mitchell, a professor of sciences from the University of North Carolina, first visited the Black Mountain Range to determine its measurements. By means of barometric readings on several of the high points, he determined that the Blacks, rather than Mt. Washington of New Hampshire, represented the top elevation in the east. Dr. Mitchell's work continued until 1857, when he fell to his death at Mitchell's Falls on the north side of the Blacks, as he sought to prove that Mt. Mitchell was the highest peak of all.

Today Mt. Mitchell is noted for the decline of the spruce and fraser fir forest that once covered its summit. Although it is well known that many of the trees succumbed to insect damage from the Balsam Wooly Adelgid, many people believe that air pollution is also a factor.

The following activities will encourage your students to consider the history of this famous peak, follow logging practices here, and make some conclusions about environmental threats to the area.

Mt. Mitchell, a North Carolina State Park, is only accessible from the Blue Ridge Parkway at milepost 350 — about an hour north of Asheville. The closest state road access is where Route 80 intersects the Blue Ridge Parkway, between Marion and Burnsville, NC. For further information, call the park at (704) 675-4611.

DR. ELISHA MITCHELL

GOAL:
The goal is for the students to realize that the story of Dr. Elisha Mitchell is true and a part of American history.

OBJECTIVE:
The learner will realize the story of Dr. Elisha Mitchell is a true story. The learner will write a letter asking for a pamphlet on Dr. Elisha Mitchell. The learner will write a nonfictional and a fictional story about themselves.

STRAND:
Language Arts

STATE OBJECTIVES:
NORTH CAROLINA:
GOAL 2.3: The learner will apply, extend and expand on information and ideas.
GOAL 3.2: The learner will determine the value of information and ideas.

TENNESSEE:
Identify parts of friendly letters and envelopes. Read selected materials to distinguish between fact and opinion, distinguish reality and fantasy, and distinguish fiction from nonfiction.

BACKGROUND INFORMATION:
Have students write for background information about a month before you are to visit Mount Mitchell. Ask for the publication "Dr. Elisha Mitchell and the Measuring of Mount Mitchell."

N. C. Department of Environment, Health and Natural Resources
Division of Parks and Recreation
P. O. Box 27687
Raleigh, N. C. 27611-7687

OR

Mount Mitchell State Park
Route 5 Box 700
Burnsville, N. C. 28714

ACTIVITY:
Have students write a friendly letter asking for enough publications so everyone in the class has one. Put all the letters in an envelope with a cover letter from you, or choose the best one. Upon arrival of the publications, read and discuss the material. Have students write a true story about themselves. Before going on the field trip, tell the students they will be writing another story when they return, and this time they will pretend they were the one who discovered Mount Mitchell. Tell them to be aware of the surroundings so they can give a realistic account of their fictional find.

Ask students to address the following questions in their stories:

How did you travel (mode of transportation)?

What obstacles did you encounter?

What were you wearing?

What did you eat?

What supplies did you carry with you?

What was the climate?

What plants and animals did you encounter?

HISTORY OF MOUNT MITCHELL and THE BLACK MTNS.

GOAL:
To study the impact of the lumber (logging) industry on the Black Mountain Range and Mount Mitchell. To be aware of the relationship between the history of a region and its location.

STATE OBJECTIVE:
NORTH CAROLINA:

5.3: Analyze causes and consequences of the misuse of the physical environment and propose alternatives

BACKGROUND INFORMATION:
Beginning in the 1870's, northern speculators and outside businessmen carved out huge domains in the rich timberlands of the Appalachians. By 1910 outlanders controlled the best strands of hardwood and a large percentage of the surface land in the region.

More than 75% of the land came under the control of 13 corporations. One timber company alone owned more than one-third of the total acreage. These companies came in, cut the forests and left without any thought to the damage they left behind. Watersheds were damaged, there was no ground cover to hold the rainwater, and many damaging floods occurred. These logging operations left only a small portion of timber in the Black Mountains untouched.

But to a considerable degree the land did recover, and spruce and fir trees once again took hold, although in a lesser degree. The logging operations of the early twentieth century proved to be the greatest threat the Black Mountains had experienced. But out of this threat to the range's integrity, a state park was established, and on March 3, 1915, a new era of tourism began.

PRE-SITE ACTIVITIES:
Have students do research on the logging industry in the mountains. Assign groups or individual students the following topics.

I. The early history of logging 1800-1850
   A. How were the logs used?
   B. How were they cut and transported?
   C. How much was paid for the lumber?

II. The logging industry from 1850-1900
   A. What changes took place in the industry and country?
   B. What changes occurred in transportation?
   C. Who profited from the industry?

III. The logging industry from 1900-1950
   A. The movement to protect the mountains from exploitation.
   B. The early leaders of the movement.
   C. The establishment of a state park.

IV. The history from 1950-1955
   A. The growth of tourism good or bad?
   B. The new dangers of acid rain on Balsam Wooly Aphids.
   C. The future?

V. Elisha Mitchell
   A. The man.
   B. His work.
   C. The controversy between Mitchell and Clingman.

HISTORY OF MOUNT MITCHELL and THE BLACK MTNS.

VOCABULARY

BLACK MOUNTAIN

MOUNT MITCHELL

WINDFALL

LOGGING INDUSTRY

TRAIN (TWEETSIE)

BIG TOM WILSON

ELISHA MITCHELL

THOMAS L. CLINGMAN

BALSAM WOOLY APHID

ACID RAIN

FOREST FIRE

SPRUCE

FIR

HEMLOCK

STATE PARK

ON-SITE ACTIVITIES:

WINDFALLS

Windfalls are a dominant feature near the crest of the Black Mountains. Many people owe their existence to the logging industry of the early 20th century. Logging and resulting forest fires exposed the uncut forest to the full force of strong winter winds that frequent higher elevations. This began the windfall process. Windfalls are gradually pushed up-slope until they reach the height of a ridge. Several windfalls can be observed from the top of Mount Mitchell.

1. Have students locate windfalls visible from the top of the mountain. Have them sketch these windfalls. Have them note other evidence of man's effect on the environment.

2. Have students note all evidence of damage to the biome (ice, wind, etc.).

POST-SITE ACTIVITIES:

1. Using a topographic map, have students locate wind gaps.

2. Have students suggest solutions to the problems they observed.

3. Have students write letters to their local representative asking for his/her support to continue funding for Mount Mitchell State Park.

4. Have students design an advertising campaign to support and preserve the park and its biome.

5. Have students write public service announcements to support the park.

AIR-POLLUTION DETECTIVE

GOAL:
Identify environmental concerns of a local community.

STATE OBJECTIVES:
NORTH CAROLINA:

SCIENCE:

2.7.5: Recognize how humans must care for the environment to ensure animals and plants remain healthy.

The learner will construct an air pollution indicator and monitor various sites to determine types of pollutants.

INTRODUCTION:
Scientists are still trying to determine what factors are responsible for the destruction of the forests on Mount Mitchell. The massive dying of the Fraser Fir and Red Spruce trees has increased at a rate of 30% over the last several years. Research indicates a correlation between air pollution and forest decline. Eight out of ten days, Mount Mitchell is covered in clouds and fog that is sometimes as acidic as vinegar.

MATERIALS:
5 strips of oaktag per student/group (10 x 25 cm)
5 pieces of string per student/group (15 cm long)
Nickels (to trace around)
Activity and data sheets
Tape
Scissors
Ruler
Hole punch
Hand lenses

ACTIVITY:
Students may work individually or in small groups.

After visiting Mount Mitchell, students construct air-pollution indicators to test other areas for air pollution. Follow the directions below. Students record information on data charts.

Location	Time exposed	Observations

1. Cut five strips of oaktag (10 x 25 cm). Punch a hole in one end of each strip.

2. Cut five pieces of string 15 cm long. Put a piece of string through the hole in each oaktag strip. Tie the string to make a loop for hanging the strip.

3. Fold each strip in half lengthwise. Trace five nickel-sized circles in a row on the top half of each strip. Cut out the circles.

4. Put tape on the outside of each strip so the sticky side of the tape shows through the holes in the strip. Then fold the strip in half to cover the holes. Seal with tape.

5. Find a different place to hang each strip, both inside and outside. Label each strip with the location where you are going to hang it.

6. Open the strips so the sticky part of the tape is exposed. Hang the strips in the locations you chose. Note the time when you hang each strip.

7. The next day, collect the strips. As you collect each strip, fold up the bottom again and seal it.

8. Return to your classroom. Use a hand lens to observe any particles that collected on the tape. Record your observations in the chart.

DISCUSSION:
1. What did you observe on the strips?

2. Where did you find the least air pollution?

3. Can you tell if there are different types of air pollutants?

4. How can you reduce air pollution in these locations?

CLIMB EVERY MOUNTAIN

GOAL:
The learner will collect, organize and display data to show relationships of elevation to plant life and human resource uses.

STATE OBJECTIVES:
NORTH CAROLINA:

MATHEMATICS:

Goal 4: The learner will understand and use standard units of metric and customary measure.

4.11: Formulate and solve meaningful problems involving length, time and temperature and verify reasonableness of answers

Goal 6: The learner will demonstrate an understanding and use of graphing, probability and statistics.

INTRODUCTION:

The Black Mountains were once grander than the present-day Rockies of the West, but erosion has taken its toll on these mountains. Despite wear and tear over the centuries, the Black Mountains still include the highest mountain east of the Mississippi River, Mount Mitchell.

Though there was controversy during the mid-1800's over accurate measurement of the peaks, Mount Mitchell is considered the tallest at 6,684 feet. Mount Mitchell, named for Elisha Mitchell, the scientist credited with the determination of the mountain's claim to fame, is but one of several high peaks located between Boone and Asheville, North Carolina.

ACTIVITY #1

Find the elevation of each mountain listed then rank them from highest to lowest. Place each mountain peak, with its elevation, on the map of the Blue Ridge Parkway from Boone to the Asheville area.

Mountain	Height	Ranking
Grandfather Mountain	_____	_____
Hawksbill	_____	_____
Roan Mountain	_____	_____
Tablerock Mountain	_____	_____
Mount Mitchell	_____	_____
Mount Pisgah	_____	_____

ACTIVITY #2:

Mountains and forests have a unique relationship. Certain trees like to grow at certain elevations. Sketch an outline of a mountain and label the following elevations:

Above 5500	Spruce/Fir
3500-5500	Northern Hardwood Forests (Beech, Sugar Maple, Yellow Birch, Eastern Hemlock)
1500-4500	Cove Hardwood (Deciduous) Forests
Below 3500	Oak-Hickory Forests (Black Oak, White Oak, Red Oak)

POST-SITE ACTIVITIES:

1. Study topographical maps, elevation markings, etc.

2. Have the students make an elevation map of one of the mountains of the Black Mountain group.

3. Report on how Clingman and Mitchell established the elevations using a barometer.

4. Find out how topographers determine elevation today.

CLIMB EVERY MOUNTAIN

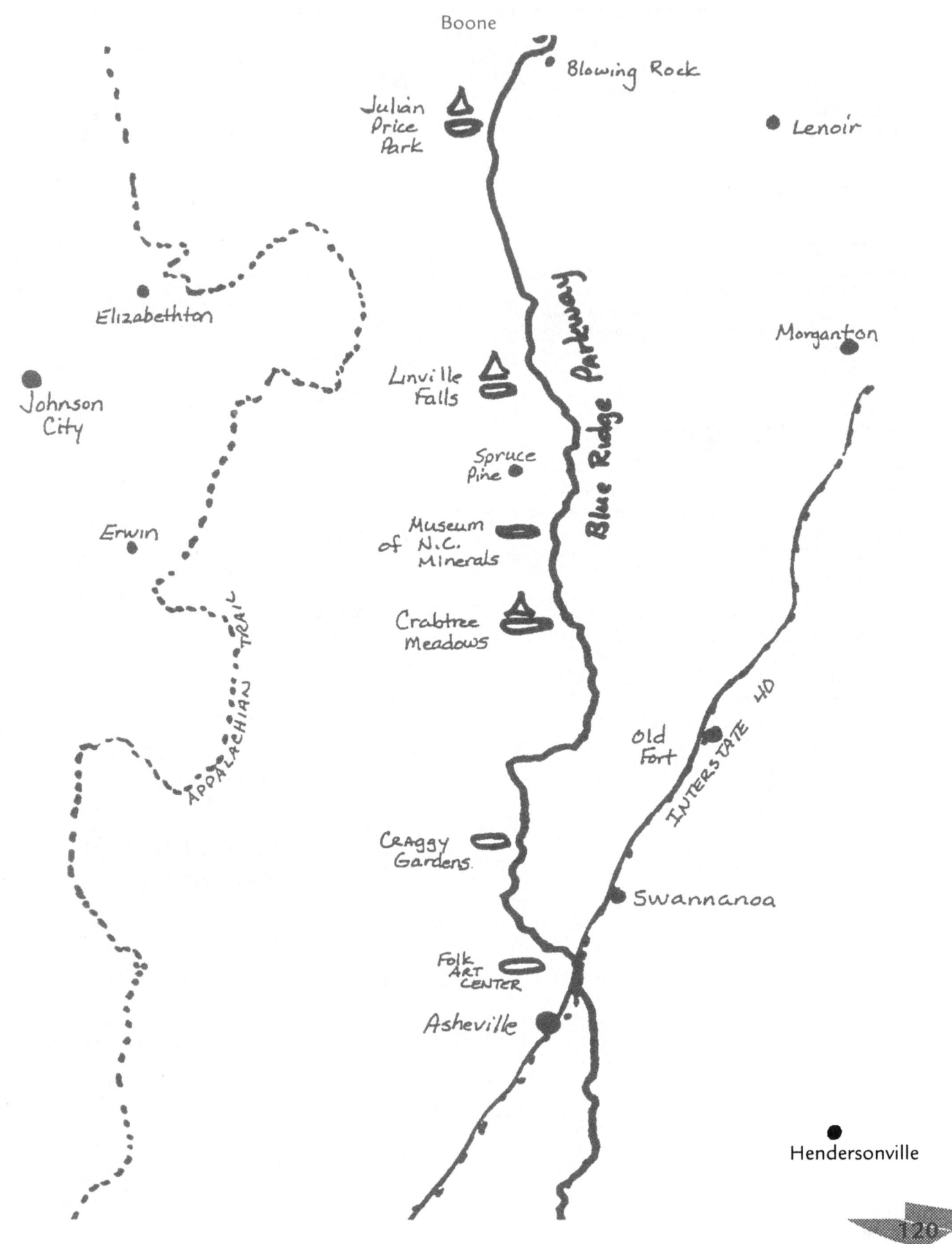

CLIMB EVERY MOUNTAIN

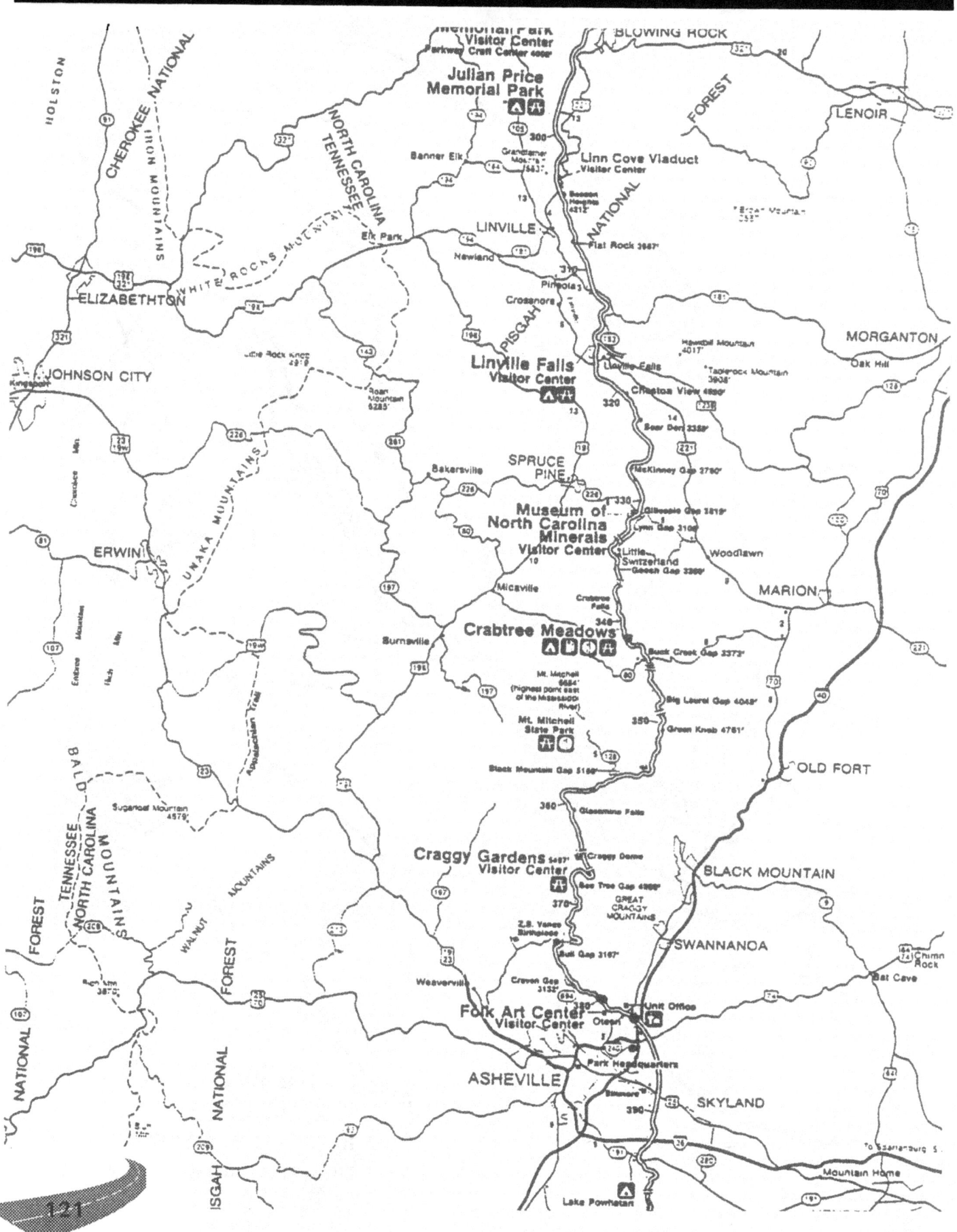

CLIMB EVERY MOUNTAIN

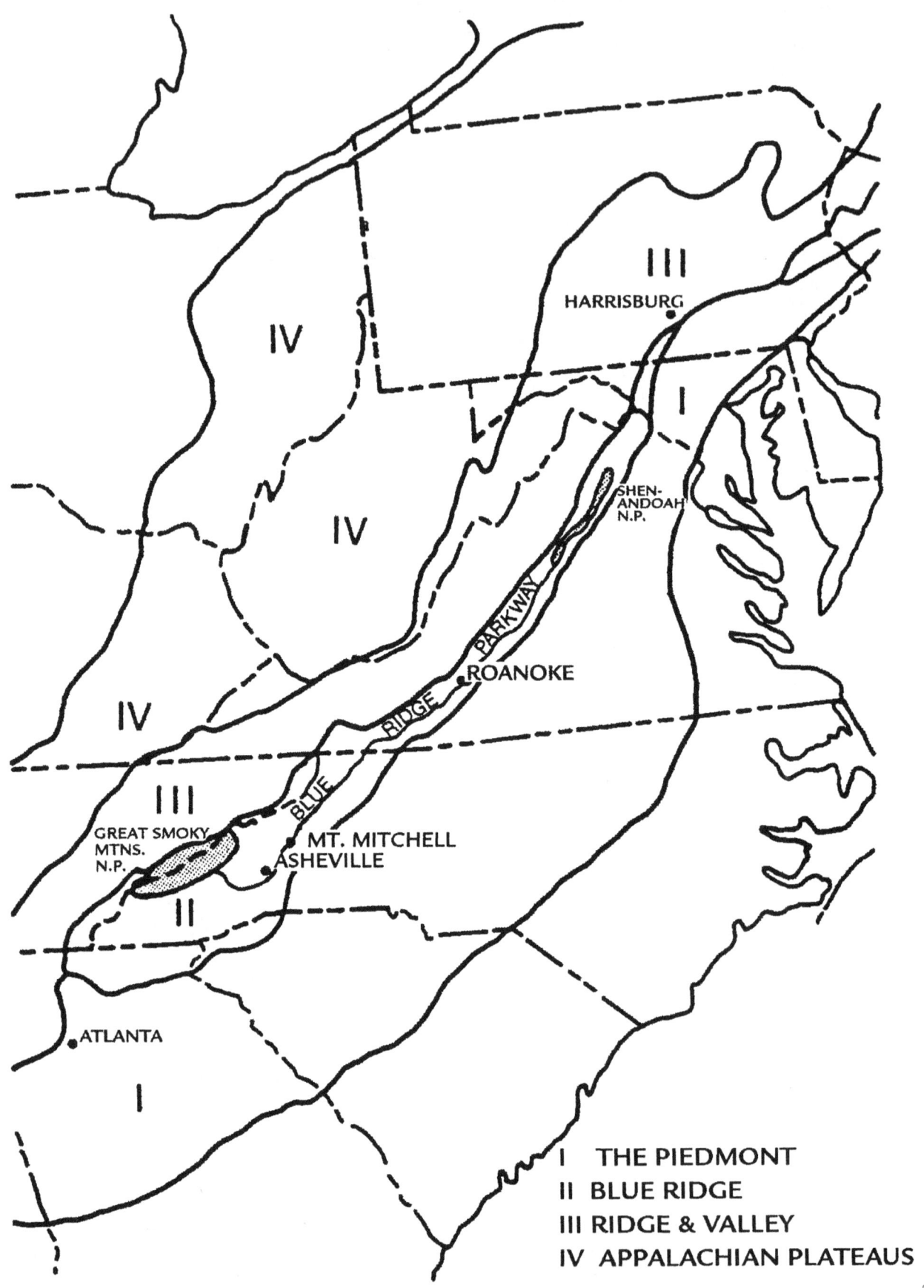

I   THE PIEDMONT
II BLUE RIDGE
III RIDGE & VALLEY
IV APPALACHIAN PLATEAUS

MOUNT MITCHELL WORD SEARCH

```
L U R D I H P A Y L O O W A O Z I K N M
V F V A N E Z C Q B H M I N I N G A O R
K Y H R Z F C D F L L A F D N I W M I Z
R E W O T A K C L I N G M A N S J I T M
R D I K R I F R E S A R F W S S G N A O
Q L D A O R L I A R K O F O Q X Q E T U
K R Z C Y X O R M D A S C X N B S R S N
J V H I Z C P Y G K J F D Q R I D A R T
C J G W O B W H R E T E M O R A B L E M
J P W S T F V I W A E M Y R B O R S H I
I C W E I R C N G N I G G O L F C S T T
G H Z C U O E I M N K B A L S A M I A C
A A O V A N I A R D I C A N I N T D E H
Y G G F D K I Z T T N T R G W I F S W E
E S E L E V A T I O N C U B M H G H W L
F I O B S E R V A T I O N M K S D M D L
F P Y L H E K S C C A S U S B I P I Y K
C D V H W E N F V J Q S T O U R I S M V
H Z A Y B L A C K M O U N T A I N S I M
C H Z O G A U R X N R J J N V F X J J R
```

WORD LIST

- ACIDRAIN
- BLACKMOUNTAINS
- FRASERFIR
- MINING
- PISGAH
- TOURISM
- WINDFALL
- BALSAM
- CLINGMAN
- LOGGING
- MOUNTMITCHELL
- RAILROAD
- TOWER
- WOOLYAPHID
- BAROMETER
- ELEVATION
- MINERALS
- OBSERVATION
- SUMMIT
- WEATHERSTATION

_____   _____   _____   _____   _____
_____   _____   _____   _____   _____
_____   _____   _____   _____   _____

MOUNT MITCHELL WORD SEARCH ANSWERS

```
. . . D I H P A Y L O O W . . . . . N .
. . . . . . . . . . . M I N I N G . O .
. . . . . . . . . L L A F D N I W M I .
R E W O T . . C L I N G M A N . . I T M
. . . R I F R E S A R F . . . . N A O
. . D A O R L I A R . . . . . . E T U
. . . . . . . . . . . . . . . . R S N
. . . . . . . . . . . . . . . . A R T
. . . . . . R E T E M O R A B L E M
. . . . . . . . . . . . . . . . S H I
. . . . . . . G N I G G O L . . . T T
. H . . . . . . . B A L S A M . A C
. A . . . N I A R D I C A . . . T . E H
. G . . . . . . . . . . . . . I . . W E
. S E L E V A T I O N . . . M . . . . L
. I O B S E R V A T I O N M . . . . . L
. P . . . . . . . . . U . . . . . . .
. . . . . . . . . . . . . S T O U R I S M .
. . . . . B L A C K M O U N T A I N S . .
. . . . . . . . . . . . . . . . . . . .
```

WORD LIST

ACIDRAIN	BALSAM	BAROMETER
BLACKMOUNTAINS	CLINGMAN	ELEVATION
FRASERFIR	LOGGING	MINERALS
MINING	MOUNTMITCHELL	OBSERVATION
PISGAH	RAILROAD	SUMMIT
TOURISM	TOWER	WEATHERSTATION
WINDFALL	WOOLYAPHID	

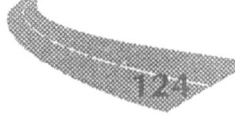

MAN and NATURE

GOALS:
The learner will evaluate ways the people of North Carolina use, modify and adapt to the physical environment. The learner will develop an understanding of the nature of science. The learner will use language for critical analysis and evaluation.

STATE OBJECTIVES:
North Carolina:
SOCIAL STUDIES:
5.3: Analyze causes and consequences of the misuse of the physical environment and propose alternatives.

SOCIAL STUDIES:
5.3.3: Given an environmental problem, predict the short-term and long-term consequences if nothing were done and propose alternatives to doing nothing.

LANGUAGE ARTS:
The learner will determine the value of information and ideas.

SCIENCE:
1.1: Show that scientific knowledge is public.
1.2: Recognize that science is historic.
1.4: Recognize that scientific knowledge is tentative.
1.5: Demonstrate that science is probabilistic.

TENNESSEE:
SOCIAL STUDIES:
Be aware of the relationship between the history of a region and its location, natural setting, natural resources and natural changes. Identify ways people pollute the land, water and air.

SCIENCE:
Realize that chemicals may be harmful to the environment. Identify environmental concerns of the local community. Realize how people interact with the environment.

PRE-SITE ACTIVITY:
Prepare a class matrix of "What we know, what we want to know, what we have learned" about Mount Mitchell. Discuss the concept of man versus nature and how this concept applies to Mount Mitchell.

ON-SITE ACTIVITY:
Have students take notes on the environment on Mount Mitchell. Have students sketch what they see.

POST-SITE ACTIVITY:
Read and discuss the following editorial from the Asheville Citizens Newspaper from August 1913.

"From a standpoint of commercialism, the wonderful activity of this district, felling these great monarchs of the forest, cutting them into short lengths, transporting them to the mill, cutting them into lumber, distributing them in the various building channels, affords a scene of intense interest and thrills the being with a sense of development and progress, turning nature's resources into money — the man — created standard of values.

Think of it! Within another twelve months the magnificent forests of spruce and balsam on the slopes of Mount Mitchell, the highest point east of the Rockies, 6,711 feet and pride of the entire eastern section of the United States will fall before the axe of the lumberman to be turned into money!"

DISCUSSION:
1. What is the writer referring to by "these great monarchs of the forest?"
2. Was the writer making a prediction about the future?
3. According to the writer, what was the relationship between man and nature?

POST-SITE ACTIVITY:
Have students write their own editorial about the conditions at Mount Mitchell, including possible solutions to the problems. Students can make dioramas that depict the physical environment of Mount Mitchell today and what it might have looked like 150 years ago.

A QUILT IS THE QUILL

GOAL:
To determine the significance of Elisha Mitchell's work and its effect on modern geographic understanding.

OBJECTIVE:
To evaluate the work of Elisha Mitchell and Thomas Clingman

STATE OBJECTIVES:
NORTH CAROLINA:
LANGUAGE 2 The learner will collect, identify, or select information and ideas

3:1 The learner will assess the value and accuracy of information

TENNESSEE:
LANGUAGE:2: The learner will identify relevant information in a paragraph

PRE-SITE ACTIVITY:
Working in teams or pairs have the students research material on Thomas Clingman and Elisha Mitchell, Clingman's Dome and Mount Mitchell. They will need to include the following: location, county and mountain range; exact height and controversy regarding height; vegetation type and animal life common and distinct; a brief history of both mountains; background information on both Clingman and Mitchell.

After having spent time on the topic, have the students prepare questions and write background for a debate; then allow students to choose sides (if the sides are uneven the teacher will need to intervene); allow time to prepare then select a representative to debate the issue with the other team. This is a good time to tie into political debates that go on in election years.

ON-SITE ACTIVITY:
As students tour the site and visit the museum have them keep a journal of all the plants (make drawings of what they see also) and animals that they observe. If any questions come up have them record those also. The journals will be discussed upon return to the class. If students have a camera or the school has a video camera this would help with a video or picture record of the trip. Students could write a script OR go with the video or picture journal with comments.

POST-SITE ACTIVITY:
Have the students design a travel brochure describing the feature they liked best, or have them tell the story of Mount Mitchell by designing a quilt; design and color each square, then put them together for a class quilt and history of the trip.

SUGGESTED BOOKS:
Western NC: Its Mountains and Its People
by Or Blackman

A History of Mt. Mitchell and the Black Mountains
by S. Kent Schwarzkoph

FIELD TRIP FORMS

We're Going on a Field Trip!

Our class is going to _____ on _____. We will
                  DATE
leave at _____ and return at
        TIME
_____. Please sign if I have
  TIME
permission to go.

_____   _____
CHILD'S NAME   PARENT'S SIGNATURE

Note to teacher: Before duplication have your students autograph the card. Be sure to sign your name also. Make enough copies to last throughout the year. When a student is absent, place a bright foil star beside his or her name and send the card home.

FIELD TRIP FORM

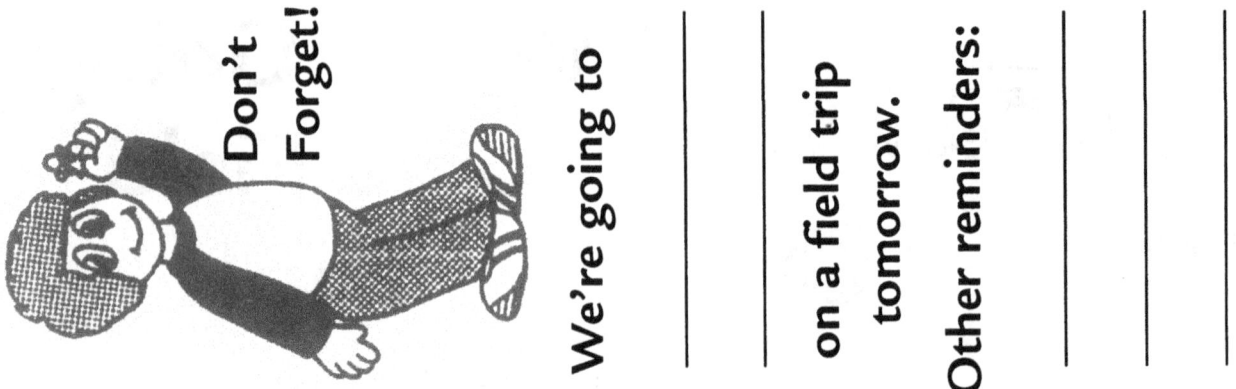

Don't Forget!
We're going to _____ on a field trip tomorrow.
Other reminders: _____ _____ _____

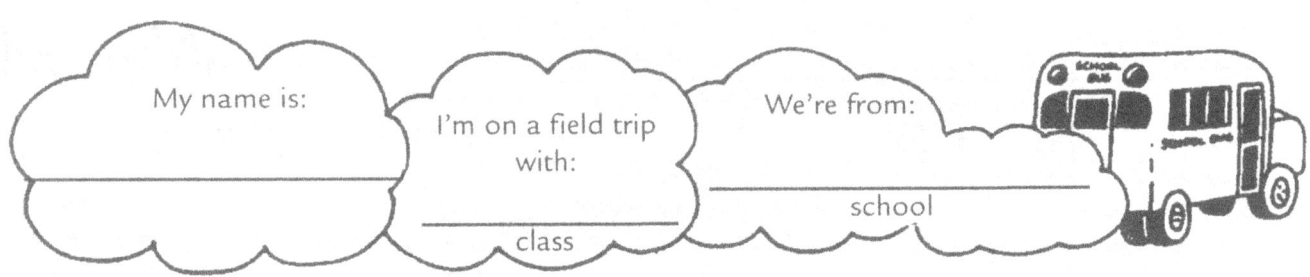

My name is: _____
I'm on a field trip with: _____ class
We're from: _____ school

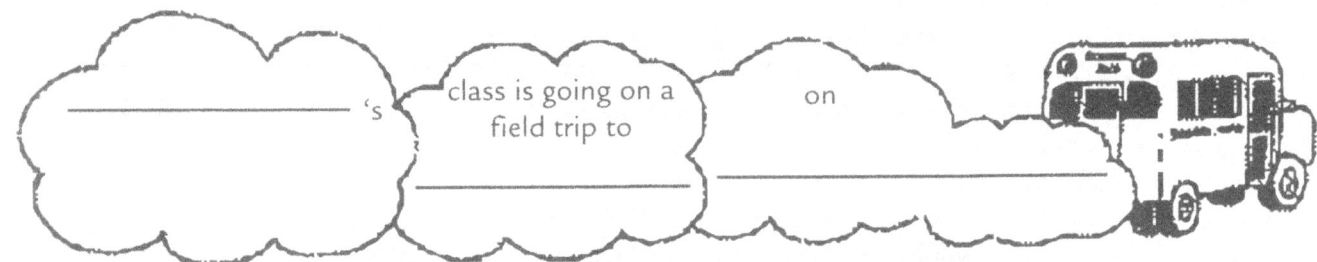

_____'s class is going on a field trip to _____ on _____

Field trip form

We plan to leave school at _____ and return at _____.

Your child will need to bring $_____ by _____ to pay for _____. Dress your child for the trip.

Other important notes _____.

- ☐ I would like to be a chaperone on this trip.
- ☐ I'm not able to be a chaperone on this trip.

Please return this signed slip by: _____

date

LUNCHTIME BEAR

LUNCHTIME IS... GRRREAT!

www.ingramcontent.com/pod-product-compliance
Lightning Source LLC
Chambersburg PA
CBHW081327190426
43193CB00043B/2813